eMuslima

A Guide to Entrepreneurial Success for Muslim Women

By Ameena Evans

Table des matières

Introduction

This comprehensive guide is your invitation to embark on a transformative journey – a journey of self-discovery, empowerment, and entrepreneurial success. Whether you have a spark of an idea or are just beginning to dream of your own venture, this guide is your roadmap to fulfillment.

For centuries, Muslim women have possessed an entrepreneurial spirit, their talents and ingenuity shaping communities and enriching lives. Today, this spirit continues to burn bright, fueled by a desire to contribute meaningfully to the world while staying true to their faith and values.

Within these pages, you will find the tools and strategies needed to navigate the exciting world of entrepreneurship. We will explore how to:

Identify business ideas that align with your Islamic values and passions

- Develop effective business plans in a Halal context

- Craft marketing strategies that resonate with both Muslim and broader audiences

- Balance your entrepreneurial aspirations with family and religious obligations

- Build a supportive network within the Muslim community and beyond

- Drawing on inspiring success stories and practical advice, this guide will equip you with the knowledge and confidence to overcome challenges, navigate cultural considerations, and turn your entrepreneurial dreams into reality.

So, sisters, take a deep breath, embrace your potential, and prepare to embark on this amazing adventure. Together, let us rise to new heights and leave our mark on the world, one successful business at a time.

Unveiling Your Entrepreneurial Calling

As a Muslim woman, your entrepreneurial spirit burns bright with a unique spark fueled by faith and purpose. You yearn to create your own path, contribute meaningfully to your community, and leave a lasting impact on the world. But how do you translate this inner desire into a thriving business that aligns with your Islamic values and fulfills your aspirations?

This journey starts with a crucial step: identifying a business idea that resonates with your core beliefs and principles. This introductory chapter will serve as your guide, illuminating the path to discovering a business concept that is not only profitable but also deeply fulfilling on a spiritual and personal level.

Through introspection, exploration, and valuable insights, we will embark on a journey of self-discovery to uncover your unique strengths and talents, those gifts that Allah has bestowed upon you and that yearn to be shared with the world.

Uncovering Your Entrepreneurial Calling: A Gift from Allah

As you embark on this journey of entrepreneurial discovery, sister, remember that your strengths and talents are not mere coincidences. They are gifts bestowed upon you by Allah, blessings waiting to be shared with the world. Just as the Prophet Muhammad (peace be upon him) said,

"The believers are like one body: if one part is in pain, the whole body feels pain,"

Your talents and gifts are intended to benefit not only yourself but also your community and the world around you.

Therefore, uncovering these strengths and talents is not merely an exercise in self-promotion, but a sacred act of discovering your unique purpose within the larger tapestry of creation. It is a journey of introspection, reflection, and connection with your inner self.

Begin by reflecting on the things you naturally excel at, the tasks you lose yourself in, and the activities that bring you joy and fulfilment. Consider the skills you have honed through education, work experience, or even your hobbies.Remember, even seemingly "ordinary" talents like cooking, organisation, or creativity can be powerful when combined with passion and a clear vision.

Take inspiration from the women who have walked this path before you. Khadija bint Khuwaylid (may Allah be pleased with her), the wife of the Prophet Muhammad (peace be upon him), was a successful businesswoman known for her intelligence, integrity, and compassion. She used her wealth and resources to support the early Muslims and played a pivotal role in the spread of Islam.

Similarly, Malala Yousafzai, the youngest Nobel Prize laureate, used her voice and courage to advocate for girls' education, inspiring millions around the world.

Think about the challenges you face in your own life and those you observe within your community. Look for unmet needs and opportunities to apply your talents to create positive change.

Remember, true success extends beyond financial gain; it lies in making a meaningful difference in the lives of others.

As you delve deeper into the well of your talents and strengths, remember that you are not alone. Seek guidance from mentors and role models, both past and present. Connect with other Muslim women entrepreneurs who can share their experiences and offer valuable insights.

Most importantly, never underestimate the power of prayer and connection with Allah. In moments of doubt or confusion, turn to Him for guidance and strength. Remember, as Allah says in the Quran,

"And whoever fears Allah - He will make for him a way out."

So, with a heart filled with faith, a mind focused on purpose, and a spirit ignited by passion, begin to unlock the unique gifts Allah has bestowed upon you. This is your calling, sister, and the world awaits your brilliance.

Unveiling Opportunities Aligned with Islamic Values

Imagine stepping into a bustling marketplace, not just any marketplace, but one teeming with possibilities and waiting to be shaped by your vision. This is the entrepreneurial landscape you are about to explore, a dynamic space where your keen eye will identify unmet needs and your creative mind will translate them into solutions that not only fulfil a purpose but also resonate with your Islamic values.

As you navigate this market, remember that your role as a Muslim woman entrepreneur transcends mere business. You are a bridge between the sacred and the secular, a conduit for change, and an ambassador of our faith.

Your business, therefore, becomes an extension of your values, a tangible expression of your commitment to ethical practices, social responsibility, and community upliftment.

This is not to say your endeavours should be confined solely to the Muslim community. Look beyond the familiar, venturing into broader markets and identifying opportunities to address universal needs through an Islamic lens.

Perhaps you notice a lack of ethical food options that cater to dietary restrictions while upholding Halal standards. Or maybe you observe a growing demand for modest clothing that is both stylish and culturally sensitive. These are just glimpses of the vast potential that awaits your discovery.

Remember, the Prophet Muhammad (peace be upon him) was himself a successful Business woman, known for his honesty, trustworthiness, and fair dealings. He emphasised the importance of understanding customer needs and providing quality goods and services. As you delve into market research, keep his wisdom close to your heart.

But don't let your research be solely quantitative. Go beyond statistics and spreadsheets. Engage with your community, listen to their voices, and understand their aspirations and frustrations.

- *What challenges do they face in their daily lives?*

- *What products or services are missing that could improve their well-being and enrich their lives?*

By combining market research with an empathetic understanding of your target audience, you will be able to identify gaps that go beyond mere market trends.

You will uncover opportunities to create solutions that are not only profitable but also ethically sound, socially responsible, and deeply meaningful for both Muslim and non-Muslim communities.

As you explore this fertile landscape of possibilities, remember that the Prophet (peace be upon him) also emphasized seeking guidance from Allah. Pray for clarity and discernment, and trust that He will guide you towards the path that best aligns with your values and brings His blessings upon your endeavors.

This exploration is not just about finding a profitable business idea, it is about finding your purpose as a business Muslim woman. It is about leaving your mark on the world and contributing to a more just and equitable society, one business at a time. So, step forward with confidence, trust in Allah, and embark on this exciting journey of discovery. The market awaits your unique vision and the world is ready to be changed.

Explore the market and identify unmet needs, seeking opportunities to fill gaps in the Muslim community or broader markets with ethical and socially responsible solutions.

Aligning Faith and Business

As I navigate the bustling marketplace, a sense of responsibility weighs heavily upon me. For I am not just a business woman, but a believer, guided by the principles of Islam that illuminate every aspect of my life. My faith is not merely a matter of private devotion; it is a compass that directs my business decisions, ensuring they remain aligned with the values of justice, mercy, and integrity that are so dear to my heart.

Each transaction, each interaction, becomes an opportunity to translate my faith into action. Honesty and fairness are not mere policies; they are the very foundation of my business dealings. I strive to uphold the highest ethical standards, ensuring that my customers are treated with respect and dignity, and that my products are of the highest quality.

But navigating the complexities of commerce while adhering to Islamic rulings requires constant vigilance and introspection. I seek knowledge from scholars of different background, immersing myself in the teachings of the Quran and the Sunnah, ensuring my understanding of permissible and impermissible practices is clear and unwavering.

There are moments of doubt, of course, when the allure of profit threatens to cloud my judgment. But in those moments, I remember the Prophet (peace be upon him), his unwavering commitment to ethical conduct even in the face of adversity.

He reminds me that true success lies not in the accumulation of wealth, but in the righteousness of one's actions and the blessings of Allah.

Therefore, I strive to be mindful of the impact my business has on the community. I prioritize responsible sourcing, ensuring that my products are not obtained through exploitative or unjust means. I support local businesses and fair trade practices, contributing to a more equitable and sustainable economy.

This journey of aligning faith and commerce is not without its challenges. But with each obstacle overcome, my resolve strengthens. I am not just building a business; I am building a legacy, one that reflects the values of Islam and leaves a positive impact on the world.

For my faith is not just a part of my life; it is the very essence of who I am. And it is this essence that guides my every step, ensuring that my journey as a Business woman is not just profitable, but also blessed and fulfilling.

Delve into your Islamic values and principles, understanding how your faith can guide your business decisions and ensure your operations remain compliant with Islamic rulings.

My sisters, we stand at a crossroads. We possess within us the spark of entrepreneurship, the desire to create, and the unwavering faith that guides our every step. But sometimes, the path forward can seem obscured, the ideal business idea elusive.

Fear not, dear sisters, for the seeds of success lie dormant within each of us, waiting to be nurtured and brought to bloom.Today, we embark on a journey of self-discovery, a quest to identify a business idea that resonates with the depths of our being and fulfills our aspirations as Muslim women.

Close your eyes, sisters, and delve into the wellspring of your desires. What are the unmet needs that tug at your heartstrings? What problems do you see in your community, in the world, that you yearn to address? Perhaps it's the lack of access to halal goods and services, the absence of culturally sensitive educational resources, or the need for a space where Muslim women can network and empower each other.

Listen to the whispers of your soul, sisters. What are the skills and talents that Allah has bestowed upon you? Are you a gifted storyteller, a skilled craftswoman, a born leader with a vision to inspire? Remember, each of these gifts has the potential to blossom into a thriving business, a beacon of hope and change in the world.

Now, open your eyes, sisters, and look around you. What are the opportunities that lie hidden within your community, within the broader world? Where are the gaps in the market that your unique skills and values can fill? Perhaps it's a modest clothing line that celebrates your faith and empowers women to feel confident and beautiful. Or maybe it's an educational platform that offers authentic Islamic knowledge and fosters a deeper connection with Allah.

Remember, sisters, your purpose goes beyond mere profit. Your business can be a tool to alleviate suffering, promote social justice, and inspire others to live according to the principles of Islam. It can be a platform to showcase the beauty and richness of our faith to the world, breaking down stereotypes and fostering understanding and collaboration.

But most importantly, sisters, let your business be an extension of your faith. Let every decision you make, every product you create, every service you offer, be guided by the values of honesty, integrity, and compassion. Remember, you are not just entrepreneurs; you are ambassadors of Islam, role models for future generations, and instruments of positive change in the world.

So step forward, sisters, with courage and confidence. Embrace your talents, harness your passion, and let your faith be your guiding light. Remember, the world needs your unique vision, your unwavering spirit, and your unwavering commitment to making a difference. The seeds of your success are waiting to be planted, the potential for positive change awaits your touch. Go forth and bloom, sisters, and may your businesses be a testament to the power of your faith and the strength of your spirit.

Craft a business idea that is both profitable and purpose-driven, creating a venture that aligns with your deepest desires and contributes positively to your community and the world.

This chapter is an invitation to embark on a transformative journey, one that will not only lead you to entrepreneurial success but also empower you to fulfill your calling as a Muslim business woman. We will navigate this path together, drawing inspiration from Islamic teachings, real-life success stories, and actionable strategies to unlock your full potential and bring your unique vision to life.

Effective Business Planning

Sisters, imagine a garden bursting with life, flourishing under the warmth of the sun and the nourishment of the soil. This garden is your business, a testament to your dedication, hard work, and unwavering faith. To ensure its growth and prosperity, a strong foundation is essential. This foundation is your business plan, a roadmap that will guide you through every challenge and lead you toward achieving your entrepreneurial dreams.

Planning your business in a Halal context is not simply a matter of outlining financial projections and marketing strategies. It is about aligning your endeavors with the principles of Islam, ensuring that every facet of your business operates with integrity, ethical conduct, and a deep commitment to social responsibility.

Sisters, as we step into the bustling world of business, we do so not only with entrepreneurial ambition, but also with the sacred responsibility of upholding the principles of our faith. Our businesses, far from being mere enterprises, become extensions of ourselves, reflecting our values and contributing to the betterment of our communities.

To ensure that our endeavors are guided by righteousness, let us delve into the wisdom of Islam, embracing key principles that will illuminate our path and guide our decisions:

- **Honesty and Integrity:** This foundation of our faith forms the bedrock of our business practices. As Allah (SWT) reminds us in the Quran,

"O you who have believed, fear Allah and be with the truthful." (Quran 9:119)

Let honesty be our hallmark, transparency our shield, and integrity our guiding light.

- **Fairness and Justice:** In the marketplace, just as in life, strive to treat everyone with fairness and justice. Remember the words of the Prophet Muhammad (PBUH):

"The best of you are those who are most beneficial to others." (Sahih Bukhari)

Let your business be a beacon of fairness, where customers and partners are treated with respect and dignity.

- **Avoiding Haram and Riba**: Our commitment to Allah (SWT) demands that we abstain from engaging in any practices deemed Haram, including Riba (usury). We actively seek knowledge and guidance from scholars to ensure our business transactions comply with Islamic rulings, safeguarding our spiritual well-being and the blessings we seek.

- **Building Trust and Relationships:** In the words of the Prophet Muhammad (PBUH):

"A believer is a mirror to another believer." (Sahih Muslim)

Let trust be the cornerstone of your business relationships. Build genuine connections with customers, suppliers, and partners, and uphold your commitments with unwavering integrity.

- **Fulfilling Needs and Serving the Community**: Our businesses are not merely profit-driven ventures; they are opportunities to serve the community and fulfill unmet needs. Whether it be providing essential goods and services, creating employment opportunities, or supporting worthy causes, let your business be a force for good in the world.

- **Seeking Allah's Guidance and Blessings**: Remember, sisters, that true success comes not only from hard work but also from the blessings of Allah (SWT). As we navigate the challenges and opportunities of the marketplace, let us constantly seek His guidance through prayer, dua, and reflection. Trust in His divine plan and know that He will reward our efforts with His bountiful blessings.

By embracing these principles, sisters, we can walk confidently in the marketplace, knowing that our businesses are not just ventures, but expressions of our faith and contributions to a better world. We can inspire others, empower our communities, and leave a legacy of righteousness and prosperity, all while earning the pleasure of Allah (SWT). May our journeys be blessed with success, both in this world and the hereafter.

Strategic Thinking

As a fellow Muslim sister and entrepreneur, I understand the profound role strategic thinking plays in our business journeys. It transcends mere skill; it becomes a guiding light, illuminating the path towards success that aligns with our values and faith. It's about carving a niche where profit and purpose intertwine, where ethical principles and market savvy dance in perfect harmony.

I can 't stop thinking of my dear friend Aisha M., a Muslim fashionista whose brand is as vibrant as her faith. Each week, she carves out sacred space for strategic reflection. Away from the daily hustle, she immerses herself in introspection. This sacred time allows her to weave Islamic values like fairness, transparency, and social responsibility into the fabric of her business. Her designs not only adorn bodies, but also uplift communities.

In your own strategic sanctuary, pause and ask yourself these potent questions:

- How does my business weave itself into the tapestry of community needs? Does it empower and uplift, or merely extract and exploit?
- Do my transactions echo the principles of Islamic ethics? Do I treat customers, suppliers, and employees with the dignity and respect they deserve?
- How can I bridge the gap between profit and purpose? Can I create a business model that thrives commercially while contributing to social good?

Remember, strategic thinking isn't a quick fix; it's a continuous voyage of self-discovery. As you navigate the entrepreneurial seas, revisiting and recalibrating your strategies becomes your compass. This constant dialogue with yourself ensures you stay true to your business vision while remaining anchored to the values that define you as a Muslim woman.

This delicate dance between success and purpose unlocks not just financial prosperity, but also a profound sense of fulfillment. It's about leaving a legacy that transcends mere numbers and products. It's about building a business that whispers your values into the world, a testament to the beautiful integration of faith and commerce.

This journey is not about erecting monuments to wealth, but about igniting beacons of impact. In this sacred pursuit, let us hone our minds into instruments of ethical change, transforming our businesses from mere enterprises into bridges that connect the whispers of community with the echoes of individual aspirations.

Remember, the compass resides within. We need only quiet the noise and listen to its gentle guidance. May our journeys be blessed with clarity, purpose, and the unwavering strength of our faith.

Avoiding Common Pitfalls

Being a Muslim sister in the dynamic world of business is an exciting adventure, but it's not without its challenges. Navigating common pitfalls can make the difference between soaring success and encountering frustrating roadblocks. So, let's unpack some of these obstacles and equip ourselves with the wisdom to gracefully overcome them:

- **The Mirage of Optimism**: While optimism is a vital fuel, unchecked enthusiasm can blur our vision. Fatima, the online halal cosmetics entrepreneur, learned this the hard way. Her initial excitement blinded her to potential market gaps and competitor strategies. Remember, a healthy dose of realistic planning and market research can turn your optimistic vision into a tangible roadmap.

- **Building on Assumptions**, Not Data: Assumptions are like quicksand – they can pull you under before you even realize it. Aisha, the catering service owner, discovered this when her menu, based on unverified assumptions about customer preferences, didn't resonate with her target audience. Data-driven decisions, informed by customer feedback and market trends, are the sturdy bridge that takes you across the chasm of uncertainty.

- **The Allure of Passive Success**: While Tawakkul, trusting in Allah's plan, is a cornerstone of our faith, it shouldn't overshadow our own responsibility to strive.

Huda, the graphic designer, initially relied solely on luck for client acquisition, but her business remained stagnant. Remember, actively networking, showcasing your skills, and diligently pursuing opportunities are essential steps on the path to success.

- **The Stagnant Learner's Trap**: The business landscape is a living, breathing thing, constantly evolving. Failing to keep up can leave you gasping for air. Joining women entrepreneur networks, attending workshops, and engaging in online learning communities can keep your knowledge and skills fresh, like a well-watered garden bursting with new blooms.

- **The Work-Life Imbalance Tightrope**: As Muslim women, juggling the demands of business with family and personal life can feel like a delicate dance on a tightrope. Neglecting any aspect can lead to a crashing fall. Fatima, after experiencing burnout from neglecting her family, learned to prioritize and schedule her time effectively, ensuring a healthy balance that nourishes all aspects of her life.

By remembering these potential pitfalls, we can approach our entrepreneurial journeys not with fear, but with informed awareness. Each challenge presents an opportunity to learn, grow, and emerge stronger – a testament to the resilience and resourcefulness of Muslim women in business. So, let's step onto this path with open hearts, sharp minds, and a unwavering faith in ourselves and the power of our dreams.

Understanding Real Problems

In the dynamic world of entrepreneurship, particularly for Muslim women, comprehending the true nature of business challenges is akin to embarking on a journey of deep exploration and understanding. It's about going beyond the superficial symptoms to unearth the underlying issues that are impacting your business. This process is reminiscent of unraveling the layers of an onion, where each layer peeled away brings you closer to the core truth.

Consider the scenario of declining sales in your business. At a cursory glance, it might seem like a straightforward marketing dilemma. However, a more in-depth examination might reveal a deeper issue such as product misalignment. This could mean that your products are no longer resonating with the evolving preferences and needs of your community. It's a reflection of the dynamic nature of markets and consumer behavior, and understanding this shift is crucial for realignment and success.

Another common issue in businesses is high employee turnover. While it's easy to dismiss this as a human resource management challenge, a more nuanced analysis might point to deeper cultural issues within the organization. This aspect is particularly vital in environments where Muslim women are employed. An inclusive, supportive, and respectful company culture isn't just beneficial for employee retention; it's essential for fostering a productive and harmonious work environment.

Cash flow problems present another instructive example. These issues are often hastily attributed to poor sales. However, the root cause might be inefficiencies in operations, or a misalignment with Islamic financial principles, which emphasize ethical and sustainable financial practices. Addressing these deeper issues can lead to more than just solving cash flow problems; it can bring about a transformative change in how the business operates, making it more efficient, ethical, and sustainable in the long run.

For Muslim women entrepreneurs, these challenges are not just business obstacles but opportunities for growth and learning. It's important to adopt a holistic, multi-dimensional view of your business. This means looking beyond immediate problems and considering the interconnectedness of various aspects of your business - from operational efficiency to company culture, and from market trends to adherence to Islamic ethics.

This comprehensive approach not only helps in effectively resolving current problems but also in building a robust, resilient business. It encourages continuous learning, adaptability, and strategic planning. By aligning your business practices with your faith and values, you not only pave the way for success in your entrepreneurial endeavors but also set a precedent for ethical and principled business leadership. This, in turn, inspires others in your community, contributing to a culture of integrity, innovation, and mutual respect in the business world.

Sisters, as we navigate the exhilarating world of entrepreneurship, let us remember the Prophet's (peace be upon him) teachings on financial wisdom. He urged us to be mindful of our spending, avoid waste, and plan for the future. In this spirit, we delve into the crucial realm of financial planning, a cornerstone upon which your business will flourish.

First, let us build a strong foundation for your financial future. Craft a comprehensive business plan that outlines your financial projections, including revenue forecasts, operational expenses, and anticipated profit margins. This plan acts as your roadmap, guiding you towards financial stability and growth.

Next, embrace the power of budgeting. Allocate your resources wisely, prioritizing essential expenses and setting aside funds for unforeseen circumstances. Remember, sisters, financial discipline is not about deprivation, but about making conscious choices that empower you to achieve your long-term goals.

Embrace innovative financial tools. Explore online resources, accounting software, and financial management apps to streamline your bookkeeping and gain valuable insights into your financial health.

Remember, knowledge is power, and understanding your financial data empowers you to make informed decisions about your business.

As your business grows, cultivate strategic partnerships. Collaborate with other Muslim entrepreneurs, seek mentorship from experienced businesswomen, and leverage the strength of your community to access funding and expertise. Remember, sisters, collaboration is not a sign of weakness, but a powerful tool for achieving collective success.

Never underestimate the power of investment. Allocate a portion of your profits back into your business. This could involve investing in new equipment, expanding your inventory, or acquiring necessary resources to propel your growth.By reinvesting, you are not only securing your financial future, but also laying the groundwork for a legacy that will benefit generations to come.

Finally, sisters, remember that financial success is not the sole measure of your journey. While it is important to be financially responsible, never lose sight of the values that guide your business. Let your faith be your compass, and remain dedicated to ethical practices, social responsibility, and contributing to the well-being of your community.

With these strategies as your guide, you will build a financially sustainable business that not only thrives in this world but also leaves a lasting impact on the world beyond. Remember, sisters, you are not alone in this journey. Walk with Allah's blessings upon your path, and together, let us build a future where Muslim women entrepreneurs stand tall, empowered and financially secure.

Demystifying Finance for the Novice Sisters

As Muslim sisters navigating the world of finance, we often encounter a sea of terms and acronyms that can feel overwhelming. Don't worry, sister! This glossary is your handy guide to understanding the key financial language:

So, let's break down some essential financial terms you should know:

Accounts Payable: Money you owe to vendors or suppliers for things your business bought. Think of it as your "I owe you" list.

Accounts Receivable: Money customers owe you for things they bought from your business. It's like an "I owe you" list in your favor!

Accrual: A fancy way of saying you record income and expenses when they happen, not just when the cash changes hands.

Amortization: Spreading the cost of intangible assets (like patents or copyrights) over their useful life. Think of it as paying off a loan for something that helps your business grow.

Annualize: Taking a financial snapshot for a shorter period (like a month) and imagining it as a whole year. It's like seeing your business's potential on a grand scale.

Asset Turnover: How efficiently your business uses its assets to generate sales. Think of it as getting the most out of what you have.

Assets: Everything your business owns, from buildings and equipment to cash in the bank. It's your "stuff."

Average Assets: The total value of your assets divided by two, giving you a middle ground picture of your financial strength.

Assets, Fixed: Tangible things you own long-term, like buildings and machinery. Think of them as your trusty tools.

Assets, Growth Rate: How much your assets have increased or decreased over a certain period. It's like a check-up on your business's growth.

Assets, Intangible: Things you own that can't be touched, like brand names or intellectual property. Think of them as your invisible assets.

Balance Sheet: A snapshot of your business's financial health at a specific point in time. It shows what you own (Assets), what you owe (Liabilities), and what you truly own (Equity).

Best in Class: The highest performance level your business has achieved in a certain area, like sales or inventory management. Aim for it, sister!

Cash Flow: The movement of money in and out of your business. Think of it as the lifeblood of your operations.

Cash Flow Statement: A report showing where your cash comes from and goes to, helping you understand your financial flow.

Capital Expenditure: Money spent on long-term assets like buildings or equipment. Think of it as an investment in your business's future.

Cost of Goods Sold (COGS): The cost of materials, labor, and overhead directly related to producing the goods you sell. It's like knowing the price tag on your products.

Current Assets: Things you can easily turn into cash within a year, like inventory or customer payments. Think of them as your readily available resources.

Current Liabilities: Money you owe within a year, like supplier bills or employee wages. Think of them as your short-term obligations.

Current Ratio: A measure of your ability to pay your short-term debts with your current assets. A higher ratio is better!

Debt: Money you borrow from others to finance your business. Remember, debt is a tool, use it wisely!

Depreciation: Spreading the cost of fixed assets over their useful life. It's like saying, "This building isn't getting any younger, let's account for it."

Dividends: A portion of your business's profits distributed to owners (shareholders). Think of it as sharing your success.

EBITDA: Earnings before interest, taxes, depreciation, and amortization. It's a measure of your business's operating profitability without external factors.

Equity: What you truly own in your business, calculated as Assets minus Liabilities. It's your net worth, sister!

Financial Statements: Documents that tell the story of your business's financial health: Balance Sheet, Income Statement, and Cash Flow Statement.

Financing Cash Flow: Money related to borrowing, repaying loans, or issuing shares. Think of it as managing your financial relationships.

Finished Goods: Products ready for sale! The fruits of your labor, sister.

Free Cash Flow: Cash generated from operations minus money spent on fixed assets. It's like your "extra" cash after running your business.

General and Administrative (G&A): Expenses like rent, utilities, and office supplies that keep your business running smoothly. Think of it as the oil in your business engine.

Gross Profit: Sales minus the cost of goods sold. It's like knowing your profit before all the other expenses come in.

Income Statement: A report showing your businesss share

Inventory: The raw materials, work-in-progress, and finished goods you have on hand. Think of it as your stockroom.

Inventory Turnover: How many times you sell and replace your inventory in a given period. A higher turnover is generally better.

Investing Cash Flow: Money used to buy or sell fixed assets or other investments. Think of it as putting your money to work for the future.

Liabilities: Money you owe to others, like creditors or suppliers. Think of them as your "IOUs."

Liquidity: Your ability to pay your short-term debts with your current assets. A higher liquidity is better!

Marketing, Selling, General, and Administrative (MSG&A): Expenses related to promoting and selling your products, as well as running your business. Think of it as the cost of doing business.

Net Cash provided by Financing Activities: The amount of cash generated or used from borrowing, repaying loans, or issuing shares. Think of it as the net inflow or outflow from your financial relationships.

Net Income: Your profit after all expenses are paid. It's the bottom line, sister!

Operating Cash Flow: Cash generated from your core business activities. Think of it as the lifeblood of your day-to-day operations.

Owners' Equity: See Equity.

Paid-in Capital: Money invested by owners or shareholders into the business. Think of it as the initial funding that set your business in motion.

Payable Days: The average time it takes you to pay your suppliers. A shorter timeframe is generally better.

Profit Margin: Your net income as a percentage of your sales. A higher margin is desirable!

Quick Ratio: A measure of your short-term liquidity, considering your most readily available assets. A higher ratio is better!

Receivable Days: The average time it takes customers to pay you. A shorter timeframe is generally better.

Receivable Turnover: How many times you collect on your accounts receivable in a given period. A higher turnover is generally better.

Retained Earnings: Profits reinvested in the business for future growth. Think of it as your seeds for tomorrow's harvest.

Return on Assets (ROA): Your net income as a percentage of your average assets. A higher ROA indicates efficient use of resources.

Return on Equity (ROE): Your net income as a percentage of your average equity. A higher ROE indicates good returns for owners.

Return on Sales (ROS): Your net income as a percentage of your sales. A higher ROS indicates profitable operations.

Solvency: Your ability to meet your long-term financial obligations. Think of it as your business's financial endurance.

Statement of Earnings: See Income Statement.

Statement of Financial Position: See Balance Sheet.

Stock: In some countries, this refers to common stock, representing ownership in a business. Think of it as your piece of the pie.

Taxes Payable: Money you owe to the government for taxes. Remember, taxes are a necessary part of running a business.

Work in Process (WIP): Inventory that's not yet finished goods. Think of it as your "almost there" products.

Remember, sister, financial knowledge is power. Use this glossary as a springboard to learn more, ask questions, and make informed decisions for your financial well-being. May your business journey be blessed with success!

ChatGPT

In today's fast-paced business world, ChatGPT is like a supercharged helper, mixing top-notch AI with real-world usefulness. It's not just great at chatting like a human – it also helps businesses connect better with customers, make their work smoother, and come up with fresh ideas. ChatGPT can take care of customer service chats, whip up cool content, sift through heaps of data really quickly and precisely, and even lend a hand in responding to emails, crafting articles, or offering basic legal advice. This tech boosts what people can do and paves the way for exciting growth and staying ahead in our ever-changing digital landscape.

Sister! AI is a powerful tool with immense potential to bless our businesses in countless ways. Let's dive into some real-world examples of how you can incorporate AI into your business, focusing on content creation:

Small businesses are leveraging ChatGPT in various innovative ways to enhance their operations and services:

- Generating Summaries: ChatGPT assists in creating concise summaries from extensive documents like meeting notes, research data, or articles, aiding in quick information digestion and decision-making.

- Creating Outlines: It helps in structuring ideas and plans by suggesting outlines based on given topics, thereby streamlining the planning process.

- SEO-friendly Keywords Generation: ChatGPT aids in identifying key SEO-friendly terms, boosting online visibility and search rankings for small businesses.

- Brainstorming Tool: The AI functions as a brainstorming partner, generating ideas for marketing strategies, social media posts, and more, thus fostering creativity.

- Automating Customer Service Emails: It automates the creation of customer service communications, such as notifications about system downtimes, holiday hours, or promotions, in multiple languages.

- Explaining Complex Concepts: ChatGPT acts as an automated encyclopedia, explaining complex topics in various fields, which can be valuable for staff training or customer education.

- Creating Responsive Chatbots: Integration of ChatGPT-powered chatbots on business websites offers advanced, AI-driven customer interaction, enhancing customer service.

- Generating Interview Questions: It helps HR departments by generating tailored interview questions, thereby optimizing the recruitment process.

- Assisting in Web Development: ChatGPT contributes to web development by generating code and helping iterate through design options, offering a starting point for further development.

Remember, sister, AI is a powerful tool, not a replacement for your creativity and expertise. Use it to enhance your existing skills, streamline processes, and gain valuable insights.

As you will experiment and learn, you'll discover even more ways to leverage AI for your business success, InshaAllah!

25 Essential Business Tools

Sisters, In today's dynamic business landscape, stagnation is not an option. To achieve sustainable success, strategic expansion is key. And what better way to fuel that growth than by leveraging the power of cutting-edge online tools?

This curated list is your roadmap to success, packed with essential platforms designed to empower your business across various facets: marketing, sales, operations, and beyond. From data-driven insights to streamlined workflows, these tools will equip you with the competitive edge you need to conquer new markets and leave your mark on the industry.

Google Workspace: https://workspace.google.com - Cloud computing, productivity, and collaboration tools developed by Google.

Microsoft Office 365: https://www.office.com - A suite of cloud-based productivity tools including Outlook, Word, Excel, etc.

Zoom: https://zoom.us - A video conferencing tool for virtual meetings and collaboration.

Slack: https://slack.com - A messaging app for team communication and collaboration.

Asana: https://asana.com - A web and mobile app designed to help teams organize, track, and manage their work.

Trello: https://trello.com - A collaboration tool that organizes projects into boards for better task management.

HubSpot: https://www.hubspot.com - Marketing, sales, customer service, and CRM software.

Salesforce: https://www.salesforce.com - A CRM solution that brings companies and customers together.

QuickBooks: https://quickbooks.intuit.com - An accounting software package for small and medium-sized businesses.

FreshBooks: https://www.freshbooks.com - Cloud-based accounting software for small business finance management.

Shopify: https://www.shopify.com - An e-commerce platform for online stores and retail point-of-sale systems.

WooCommerce: https://woocommerce.com - An open-source e-commerce plugin for WordPress.

Canva: https://www.canva.com - A graphic design platform for creating visual content.

Adobe Creative Cloud: https://www.adobe.com/creativecloud.html - Applications and services for graphic design, video editing, web development, photography, etc.

Mailchimp: https://mailchimp.com - A marketing platform specializing in email marketing.

Hootsuite: https://hootsuite.com - A tool for managing social media, scheduling posts, and tracking analytics.

Buffer: https://buffer.com - A software for managing social networks, scheduling posts, and analytics.

Google Analytics: https://analytics.google.com - A service for tracking and reporting website traffic.

SEMRush: https://www.semrush.com - A tool for SEO, PPC, content, social media, and competitive research.

Ahrefs: https://ahrefs.com - An SEO toolset for link building, keyword research, competitor analysis, etc.

Square: https://squareup.com - Payment processing and business solutions for small to medium businesses.

Xero: https://www.xero.com - Online accounting software for small businesses.

Evernote: https://evernote.com - An app designed for note taking, organizing, task management, and archiving.

Dropbox: https://www.dropbox.com - A file hosting service offering cloud storage, file synchronization, and client software.

SurveyMonkey: https://www.surveymonkey.com - An online survey development cloud-based software as a service company.

Each of these tools offers unique functionalities that can help streamline various aspects of business operations, from productivity and project management to marketing and financial management.

Building a Strong Team for Your Journey

Sisters, as we embark on this noble endeavor of entrepreneurship, let us remember again the Prophet's (peace be upon him) emphasis on community and collaboration. He said,

"The believers are like one body, when one part is in pain,

the whole body suffers with it."

For Muslim sisters in business, building a team is about more than just hiring skilled individuals. It's about creating a harmonious group of 'A' players who embody commitment, accountability, and skill, all while resonating with the values and ethics of your business.

Imagine you're launching a new product line in your business. You need a team that not only has the technical skills but also understands and respects the cultural and ethical considerations important to your customer base. This could include a marketing expert who is adept at crafting messages that resonate with your community, a product designer who is aware of Islamic principles and aesthetics, and a customer service representative who understands the nuances of your market.

In team building, consider the diverse skill sets and backgrounds that each member brings to the table. A mix of talents and perspectives can foster innovation and creativity. For instance, having a team member who is skilled in eco-friendly practices can help align your business with the Islamic principle of stewardship over the environment.

Your team should also reflect the principles of fairness, integrity, and respect, core tenets of Islamic ethics. This means creating a workplace culture where every team member feels valued, heard, and motivated to contribute their best.

In essence, building a team as a Muslim woman entrepreneur is about more than just skills; it's about cultivating a group of individuals who share your vision, uphold your values, and are committed to the collective success of your business.

This holds true for our entrepreneurial journeys as well. We cannot achieve success alone, but must surround ourselves with individuals who share our values and can contribute their unique skills and expertise.

Consider this: when the Prophet (peace be upon him) migrated to Medina, he established a strong team of advisors and supporters. He consulted with them, relied on their strengths, and delegated tasks according to their abilities. This collective wisdom and collaborative spirit were instrumental in building a thriving community and laying the foundation for the Islamic empire.

Similarly, sisters, we must build a team that will support us on our entrepreneurial paths. Look for individuals who possess the following qualities:

- **Shared values**: Surround yourself with individuals who understand and respect your Islamic values and principles.This ensures that your business decisions are guided by ethical and moral considerations.

- **Complementary skills**: Seek out individuals who bring different skills and expertise to the table. This could be a marketing expert, a financial advisor, a web developer, or anyone whose talents complement your own.

- **Trustworthiness and loyalty:** Build your team with individuals who are reliable, honest, and dedicated to your vision. These are the pillars of a strong and supportive network.

- **Positive and encouraging**: Choose individuals who believe in you and your dreams. Their positive energy and encouragement will fuel your motivation and help you overcome challenges.

- **Open communication and collaboration**: Foster an environment of open communication where team members can share ideas, offer constructive criticism, and work together towards a common goal.

Remember, sisters, building a strong team is an investment in your own success. By surrounding yourself with the right individuals, you can leverage their strengths, overcome challenges, and achieve your entrepreneurial goals.

Here are some practical ways to build your team:

Network with other Muslim entrepreneurs. Attend industry events, join online communities, and connect with individuals who share your values and understand your challenges.

Seek mentorship from experienced business professionals. Find individuals who can offer guidance, advice, and support as you navigate the entrepreneurial landscape.

Delegate tasks and responsibilities. Don't try to do everything yourself. Identify areas where you need help and delegate tasks to individuals who possess the necessary skills and expertise.

Offer opportunities for professional development. Invest in your team's growth by providing them with learning opportunities, training programs, and resources to enhance their skills.

Build a culture of appreciation and recognition. Acknowledge the contributions of your team members and celebrate their achievements. This fosters a positive and supportive work environment.

Sisters, let us remember that building a strong team is not just about achieving financial success. It is about creating a network of support, a community of like-minded individuals who will empower us to fulfill our entrepreneurial aspirations while remaining true to our values. By collaborating, supporting one another, and sharing our knowledge and resources, we can create a powerful force for positive change in the business world.

So, sisters, go forth and build your teams. Inspire one another, and leave a lasting legacy as successful Muslim women entrepreneurs who not only built businesses but also built a community of support and empowerment for generations to come.

Embracing Emotional Intelligence

It's a common perception that women tend to be more emotionally expressive compared to men. This trait, often viewed through a narrow lens, can actually be a formidable strength, especially in the business world. Women's emotional depth and empathy can foster a more inclusive, understanding, and responsive business environment. This emotional intelligence enables women to be acutely aware of the needs and feelings of both employees and customers, allowing for a more nuanced approach to leadership and customer relations.

In negotiation and conflict resolution, these emotional insights can be invaluable, offering a broader perspective that goes beyond mere facts and figures. Women's ability to empathize and connect on a deeper level can lead to more sustainable and mutually beneficial business relationships.

Moreover, this emotional acuity can drive innovation. Understanding people's emotional drivers can inspire new ideas, products, or services that better meet customer needs. Women's emotional sensitivity, when harnessed correctly, is not a weakness but a powerful tool in the competitive world of business. It allows for a leadership style that is compassionate, intuitive, and effective, underscoring the importance of emotional intelligence alongside analytical and strategic thinking.

Running a successful business often involves navigating a tightrope between data and intuition, especially for Muslim women entrepreneurs who strive for both ethical practices and financial stability. While emotions can be powerful motivators, grounding decisions in careful analysis, market research, and clear goals leads to more sustainable success.

Imagine a clothing brand experiencing a surprising dip in sales. An emotional response might be to panic-discount everything, potentially harming brand perception and profitability. Instead, a strategic approach would involve analyzing sales data, understanding customer feedback, and exploring trends to inform adjustments that align with the brand's values and long-term vision.

Similarly, managing a challenging employee situation can be emotionally charged. Rushing to a quick resolution might feel cathartic but could be detrimental in the long run. A strategic approach prioritizes open communication, objective performance evaluations, and a consideration of all stakeholders' needs. This ensures a fair and just outcome that benefits both the individual and the company's well-being.

Embracing both strategic thinking and emotional intelligence allows Muslim women entrepreneurs to navigate the complexities of business with grace and wisdom. By grounding decisions in facts and data while acknowledging the power of intuition and empathy, they can build thriving businesses that align with their ethical values and achieve sustainable success.

Understanding Emotional Intelligence

As Muslim sisters navigating the world, we wear many hats. We strive to be strong and resilient, yet nurturing and compassionate. We balance our faith with our ambitions, and our family with our careers. In this delicate dance, emotional intelligence (EQ) becomes a powerful tool, helping us navigate life's challenges and build meaningful connections.

So, what is EQ exactly? Imagine it as a bridge connecting our thoughts and feelings. It's the ability to understand and manage our own emotions, while also perceiving and responding sensitively to the emotions of others. It's not just about being "good with feelings"; it's about harnessing them to navigate life with wisdom and grace.

Why is EQ important?

- Strengthening faith and practice: EQ helps us cultivate self-awareness, a key aspect of self-reflection and spiritual growth. By understanding our emotions and triggers, we can make conscious choices that align with our Islamic values.

- Building stronger relationships: EQ allows us to empathize with others, fostering understanding and compassion within our families, communities, and business dealings. We can build bridges of communication and resolve conflicts with respect and kindness.

- Making wise decisions: EQ helps us navigate complex situations with clarity and discernment. We can avoid impulsive decisions driven by emotions and instead make choices based on reason, Islamic principles, and long-term goals.

- Fostering mental well-being: By managing our own emotions effectively, we can build resilience against stress, anxiety, and negativity. We can create a space of inner peace and tranquility, even amidst life's challenges.

Developing your EQ:

- Practice self-awareness: Observe your own thoughts and feelings without judgment. Notice your triggers and how they affect your behavior.

- Embrace the power of dua and reflection: Turn to prayer and mindfulness practices to connect with your inner self and seek guidance from Allah.

- Develop active listening skills: Pay attention to what others are saying and feeling, both verbally and non-verbally. Show empathy and understanding.

- Communicate assertively: Express your needs and opinions clearly and respectfully, while also being open to hearing different perspectives.

- Seek knowledge and support: Learn about EQ from Islamic resources and reliable sources. Connect with other Muslim sisters who can offer support and guidance on your journey.

Remember, developing EQ is a continuous process. Be patient with yourself, celebrate your progress, and don't hesitate to seek support when needed. As you cultivate your emotional intelligence, you'll discover a deeper understanding of yourself, stronger connections with others, and a more fulfilling journey as a Muslim sister.

May Allah guide you on your path to emotional intelligence and illuminate your way with wisdom and grace.

Marketing with Integrity

Sisters, as we embark on this entrepreneurial journey, let us remember that our success is not solely measured by profit margins and market share. A Muslim woman making a difference through entrepreneurship understands that her business is an extension of her faith, a platform to not only uplift herself but also contribute to the well-being of her community. And it is within this context that marketing becomes more than mere sales tactics; it becomes a tool for ethical engagement, building trust, and fostering positive change.

So, how do we navigate the world of marketing while upholding our principles and staying true to Islamic values? Here are some strategies to guide your path:

- **Transparency**: Be open about your products or services. This includes clear information about pricing, any limitations, and honest advertising without misleading claims.

- **Respect for Privacy**: Implement strict privacy policies to protect customer data. Always seek consent before using customer information for marketing purposes.

- **Truthful Advertising**: Ensure that all advertising content is truthful and does not exaggerate the capabilities of the product or service.

- **Sustainable Practices**: Adopt and promote eco-friendly practices in production and packaging, showing commitment to environmental sustainability.

- **Fair Pricing**: Price products and services fairly, offering good value without exploiting customers, especially in markets with less competition.

- **Cultural Sensitivity**: Be aware of and respect cultural differences in marketing campaigns to avoid stereotypes or offending diverse audience groups.

- **Supporting Social Causes**: Align with social causes or charities that resonate with your brand values, contributing a portion of profits to these causes.

- **Non-Deceptive Packaging**: Design packaging that accurately reflects the product inside, avoiding oversized packages that give an illusion of more content.

- **Inclusivity**: Ensure marketing materials reflect diversity in terms of race, gender, age, and abilities, promoting inclusivity.

- **Honest Testimonials and Endorsements**: Only use genuine customer testimonials and ensure influencers or endorsers genuinely use and endorse the product.

- **Avoiding Fear Tactics**: Steer clear of marketing that plays on consumers 'fears or insecurities, focusing instead on positive messaging.

- **Quality Assurance**: Maintain high-quality standards for products or services to ensure customer safety and satisfaction.

- **Employee Advocacy**: Treat employees well and encourage them to be brand advocates, reflecting the company's ethical practices internally and externally.

- **Community Involvement**: Actively participate in community events or initiatives, demonstrating social responsibility and local support.

- **Accessible Marketing**: Ensure marketing materials are accessible, including formats for people with disabilities (like captions for videos).

- **Ethical Affiliate Relationships**: Partner with affiliates who align with your brand's ethical standards and ensure they adhere to these in their promotions.

- **Clear Return and Refund Policies**: Have clear, fair, and easily accessible policies for returns and refunds, building trust with customers.

- **Balanced Competitive Strategies**: While competitiveness is necessary, avoid strategies that unfairly undermine competitors, such as spreading false information.

- **Responsible Content Marketing**: Produce content that is not only relevant and useful but also ethically sound and free from plagiarism or manipulation of facts.

Remember, sisters, marketing with integrity is not about compromising your values for short-term gains. It is about building a business that reflects your faith, contributes to the well-being of your community, and leaves a positive mark on the world. By embracing these strategies and staying true to your principles, you will become a beacon of ethical marketing, inspiring others and paving the way for a future where success is measured not just by numbers but by the positive impact we create on the world around us.

Conquering the Digital Realm

Dear Muslim Sisters, In this era of digital transformation, conquering the digital realm presents a unique and empowering opportunity, especially for us, Muslim women. This journey is not just about technology; it's about how we can use this powerful tool to carve out our space, share our stories, and connect with the world while staying true to our faith and values.

The digital world, with its vast reach, offers us an unparalleled platform to amplify our voices. We have seen how social media and online platforms have revolutionized the way narratives are shaped. It's time we leverage these tools to redefine the Muslim woman's story, often told from perspectives not our own. As Malala Yousafzai once said, "We realize the importance of our voices only when we are silenced." Now, we have the means not to be silenced.

E-commerce and online businesses are other realms where Muslim women can thrive. It's not just about financial independence, but also about bringing unique products and services that reflect our culture and values into the mainstream market. Whether it's modest fashion, halal cosmetics, or Islamic art, our contributions can diversify the global marketplace. As Ameera Al-Taweel advocates, "Women are half of society. You cannot have a healthy society without empowering all its members."

However, conquering the digital realm also means being aware of its challenges. Cybersecurity, online harassment, and data privacy are issues that we must navigate wisely. Building a secure digital presence, being conscious of the information we share, and understanding our digital rights are crucial steps in this journey.

Education and skill-building are key. Engaging with digital literacy programs, coding workshops, and online courses will equip us with the tools to not just participate but lead in the digital space. Remember, as Muslim women, our pursuit of knowledge is not just a cultural value but a religious one. The Prophet Muhammad (peace be upon him) said, "Seeking knowledge is an obligation upon every Muslim."

Collaboration and community building online is another powerful way to conquer the digital realm. By supporting each other, sharing resources, and creating inclusive online communities, we can build a strong network of Muslim women thriving in various digital fields.

In all these endeavors, let's ensure that our engagement in the digital world aligns with our ethical and religious values. The digital space is not just a mirror reflecting society; it's a canvas on which we can paint our visions and values. Let us use it to create a narrative that is authentic, powerful, and inspiring.

As we embark on this journey, let's remember that conquering the digital realm is not just about individual success. It's about creating a legacy that inspires the next generation of Muslim women to dream bigger, reach higher, and break barriers, both online and offline.

With faith, determination, and the right tools, the digital realm is not just within our reach; it's ours to lead and transform.

The Power Of Funnel

My fellow sisters, as we navigate the ever-evolving landscape of online business, we constantly seek tools to enhance our outreach, engage our audience, and ultimately, achieve our goals. Today, I want to introduce you to a powerful tool that can revolutionize your online presence: the funnel.

Think of a funnel as a bridge between your audience and your desired outcomes. Whether it's driving sales for your handcrafted jewelry line, promoting your online courses on Islamic entrepreneurship, or simply growing your community of like-minded sisters, a well-designed funnel can guide your audience through a strategic journey, increasing engagement and nurturing them towards conversion.

Here's why sisters should consider integrating funnels into their business strategy:

- Enhanced Focus and Clarity: Unlike websites, which often present a wealth of information, funnels provide a laser-focused path for your audience. This structure eliminates distractions and guides them directly towards your desired outcome, whether it's purchasing your product, subscribing to your email list, or signing up for your online course.

- Data-Driven Optimization: Funnels offer a controlled environment to track user behavior and analyze their journey step-by-step. This data-driven approach allows you to identify where users are dropping off and what elements need improvement, empowering you to continuously optimize your funnel for maximum effectiveness.

- Personalized User Experience: In today's world, a one-size-fits-all approach rarely resonates. Funnels allow you to tailor the user experience based on individual choices and actions, creating a more personalized and engaging journey that fosters trust and connection.

- Increased Conversion Rates: By streamlining the user journey and eliminating unnecessary steps, funnels significantly improve the chances of users taking the desired action, leading to higher conversion rates for your business.

- Efficient Marketing Efforts: Funnels are like well-oiled machines, guiding your audience through a pre-defined path. This automated process saves you time and resources, freeing you to focus on other aspects of your business while still achieving your marketing goals.

Implementing a funnel doesn't require technical expertise. There are numerous user-friendly tools available, along with countless resources and tutorials to guide you through the process. Remember, the key to success lies in clearly defining your goals, understanding your audience, and continuously monitoring and improving your funnel over time.

Launching Your First Funnel with ClickFunnels: A Step-by-Step Guide

Step 1: Define Your Objective

Before diving into the technical aspects, take a moment to clearly define your funnel's goal. What do you want your audience to do by the end of the journey? Is it subscribing to your email list, purchasing a product, or signing up for a course? Having a clear objective will guide every step of your funnel creation.

Step 2: Choose Your Funnel Type

ClickFunnels offers various pre-designed funnel templates to cater to different goals. Choose the one that best aligns with your objective:

- **Lead Capture Funnels**: Designed to collect email addresses and build your audience.

- **Sales Funnels**: Guide users through the sales process, culminating in a purchase.

- **Webinar Funnels**: Promote and automate webinar registrations & follow-up.

- **Membership Funnels**: Deliver exclusive content and build recurring revenue.

- **Product Launch Funnels**: Generate hype and anticipation for your product launch.

Step 3: Design Your Funnel Pages

ClickFunnels provides a user-friendly visual editor to design your funnel's landing pages. Here's a breakdown of key elements:

- **Headline**: Captivate attention and convey the value proposition.

- **Subheadline**: Expand on the headline and provide additional details.

- **Hero Image/Video**: Visually engage your audience and create a positive first impression.

- **Benefits and Features**: Clearly highlight the benefits your product or service offers.

- **Call to Action (CTA)**: Tell users what you want them to do next (e.g., subscribe, buy now).

Step 4: Integrate Email Marketing

Connect your ClickFunnels account with your preferred email marketing service (e.g., **Mailchimp**, **ActiveCampaign**) to automate email sequences based on user actions within the funnel. This allows personalized communication and nurtures leads into paying customers.

Step 5: Set Up Payment Processing

If your funnel involves selling products or services, integrate a payment gateway like **Stripe** or **PayPal** to accept online payments. This ensures a seamless checkout experience for your customers.

Step 6: Add Opt-in Forms

Prompt users to join your email list by strategically placing opt-in forms throughout your funnel. Offer incentives like free resources or exclusive content in exchange for their email address.

Step 7: Track and Analyze Performance

ClickFunnels provides detailed analytics to monitor your funnel's performance. Track key metrics like conversion rates, page visits, and customer acquisition cost to identify areas for improvement and optimize your funnel for maximum effectiveness.

Step 8: Test and Optimize

Funnels are not a "set it and forget it" solution. Continuously test different variations of your pages, CTAs, and email sequences to see what resonates best with your audience. A/B testing allows you to optimize your funnel and maximize results.

Additional Resources:

- ClickFunnels Help Center: https://help.clickfunnels.com/

- ClickFunnels YouTube Channel: https://www.youtube.com/watch?v=_SV-lllg7J0

- ClickFunnels Facebook Group: https://help.clickfunnels.com/hc/en-us/articles/360006211534-How-To-Join-The-FunnelHacker-Facebook-Community

Remember Sisters:

The advice provided here is high-level, offering a strategic overview of the effectiveness of sales funnels over traditional websites and how to implement them effectively. However, this is just the beginning of your journey. To truly master these concepts and leverage them for your success, you, my sisters, will need to dive deeper into each area.

Exploring the intricacies of sales funnels requires a commitment to continuous learning and application. It involves understanding your audience's specific needs, experimenting with different funnel strategies, and using analytics to refine your approach continually. Embrace this learning process, as it is through this deeper exploration and practical application that you will unlock the full potential of these strategies.

Remember, the digital landscape is vast and ever-evolving. Staying informed, adapting to new trends, and being willing to innovate are key to mastering digital marketing and sales funnels. Your journey to conquering this realm is both exciting and challenging, and it's in the depth of these waters that the true treasures lie.

Building a Thriving Online Community

Building a thriving online community is crucial for any business, but it's especially important for Muslim entrepreneurs who want to connect with their target audience, build brand loyalty, and foster a sense of belonging. Here are some examples of how Muslim businesses can build strong online communities:

Create Facebook Groups

Building a successful Facebook Group isn't just about clicking buttons and posting content. It's about nurturing a vibrant community, fostering meaningful connections, and providing value to your members. Here's a detailed step-by-step guide to help you create a Facebook Group that thrives:

Defining Your Purpose:

Before diving in, take a moment to crystallize your "why." What problem are you solving for your target audience? What value will your group bring to their lives? Are you offering a safe space for discussion, mentorship, or collaboration? Clearly defining your purpose will guide your content, attract the right members, and ensure your group's long-term sustainability.

Crafting an Irresistible Invitation:

Your group's name and description are your digital handshake. Make them count! Choose a name that is clear, catchy, and accurately reflects your group's focus. The description should be a concise yet compelling invitation, highlighting the benefits of joining and piquing curiosity about your community.

Laying the Ground Rules:

A thriving community needs a healthy foundation. Set clear and enforceable ground rules that promote respect, inclusivity, and productive discussion. Address common issues like spam, negativity, and self-promotion. Remember, your rules set the tone for your group's culture.

Visual Storytelling:

First impressions matter! Design an eye-catching group image and cover photo that visually represent your community's essence. Use high-quality visuals that resonate with your target audience and create a welcoming atmosphere.

Welcoming with Open Arms:

Make new members feel valued from the moment they join. Greet them personally, answer their questions, and guide them through the group's features. Consider creating a welcome post introducing yourself and outlining your group's purpose.

Content is Queen:

Engage your members with a diverse mix of content! Share informative articles, inspiring quotes, thought-provoking questions, and relevant videos. Encourage user-generated content by hosting discussions, featuring member stories, and running contests. Remember, quality over quantity is key.

Spark the Conversation:

Don't let your group become a passive audience. Encourage participation by asking open-ended questions, hosting live Q&A sessions, and organizing polls or surveys. Respond to comments and messages promptly, fostering a sense of community and belonging.

Master the Facebook Toolbox:

Facebook offers a treasure trove of features to empower your group. Pin important information to the top of the group page, schedule posts in advance, and leverage targeted ads to reach a wider audience. Utilize the "Group Insights" tool to track your group's growth and engagement, helping you tailor your content and strategies for maximum impact.

Learn and Adapt:

Building a thriving community is an ongoing process. Actively listen to member feedback, analyze data to identify trends, and be willing to adapt your approach based on your findings. Don't be afraid to experiment with different content formats and engagement strategies.

Patience and Passion:

Remember, Rome wasn't built in a day! Building a vibrant Facebook Group takes time, dedication, and a genuine passion for connecting with others. Stay consistent, be patient, and celebrate every milestone, big or small. Your passion and commitment will be contagious, attracting like-minded individuals and building a thriving community that supports and empowers its members.

So, go forth and create your Facebook Group! By following these steps, focusing on value, and embracing the power of community, you can cultivate a space for meaningful connections, mutual growth, and lasting impact.

Bonus Tip: Consider partnering with other groups or influencers in your niche to cross-promote your community and reach a wider audience.

Muslim Women Connect: https://www.facebook.com/muslimwomenconnect/ This group boasts over 600,000 members and offers a platform for Muslim women to connect, share experiences, and support each other on various topics like faith, family, and careers.

Muslim Entrepreneurs Hub: https://www.facebook.com/groups/muslimentreprene urcommunity/ This group caters specifically to Muslim entrepreneurs, providing networking opportunities, resource sharing, and mentorship for building successful businesses aligned with Islamic values.

Additional Tips:

- Use the Facebook search bar to find relevant groups using keywords like "Muslim women," "Islamic entrepreneurs," "Quran," etc.

- Look for groups with active discussions and engaged members.

- Read the group rules and descriptions carefully before joining to ensure it aligns with your expectations.

- Be respectful, contribute positively, and actively participate in discussions to become a valuable member of the community.

- I hope this gives you a good starting point for exploring and connecting with Muslim communities on Facebook. May you find valuable connections and support within these vibrant online spaces!

Utilize Instagram Stories

Creating a successful brand on Instagram, particularly for a Muslim sister audience, involves understanding and respecting cultural values while effectively utilizing Instagram's features. Here's a detailed step-by-step guide:

Understand Your Audience

- Research: Learn about the interests, needs, and values of Muslim sisters.
- Cultural Sensitivity: Ensure your content is culturally appropriate and respectful.

Define Your Brand Identity

- Unique Value Proposition: What makes your brand stand out?
- Visual Identity: Choose colors, fonts, and imagery that resonate with your audience and reflect Islamic values.
- Voice and Tone: Develop a voice that is respectful, engaging, and relatable.

Create a Content Strategy

- Content Types: Mix educational, inspirational, and promotional content.
- Consistency: Post regularly but prioritize quality.

- Engagement: Encourage interaction through questions, polls, and calls to action.

Optimize Your Instagram Profile

- Bio: Clearly state what your brand is about.
- Profile Picture: Use a logo or image that represents your brand.
- Highlights: Use Instagram Stories Highlights to categorize and showcase important content.

Utilize Instagram Features

- Stories: Share behind-the-scenes content, daily thoughts, or quick updates.
- IGTV and Reels: Create longer form and engaging video content.
- Live Sessions: Host Q&A sessions, discussions, or live product demonstrations.

Collaborate and Network

- Partnerships: Collaborate with other Muslim influencers or brands.
- Community Engagement: Regularly engage with followers and similar accounts.

Leverage Hashtags and SEO

- Relevant Hashtags: Use hashtags that are popular among your target audience.

- SEO Practices: Include relevant keywords in your captions and bio.

Monitor and Adapt

- Analytics: Use Instagram Insights to track performance.
- Feedback: Listen to your audience and adapt your strategy accordingly.

Advertise Wisely

- Targeted Ads: If you use paid ads, target them to reach the right audience.
- Promotional Offers: Share exclusive offers to your Instagram followers.

Stay Informed and Evolve

- Trends: Keep up with social media and cultural trends.
- Continuous Learning: Attend workshops, webinars, and follow industry leaders.
- Remember, authenticity and respect for your audience's values are key in building a successful brand, especially in a culturally sensitive context like this. Engage with your audience genuinely and provide value through your content.

Muslim Women Influencers on Instagram (by category):

Faith and Inspiration:

@yaalkaaaate: Inspiring content on Islamic principles and personal growth.

@ummzahrah: Authentic and relatable reflections on faith, marriage, and motherhood.

@muslimgirl: Platform for diverse Muslim voices sharing stories of faith and empowerment.

@thehijabiblogger: Beautiful visuals and insightful reflections on faith, modesty, and self-love.

@muslimahscientist: Intersection of faith and science, inspiring young Muslim women in STEM fields.

Fashion and Lifestyle:

@dina_tokiyo: Effortlessly stylish modest fashion inspiration with a global perspective.

@hautehijab: High-fashion hijab tutorials and empowering messages of self-expression.

@manaljamil: Curated modest looks and tips for everyday wear.

@themodestymovement: Platform for diverse voices and styles within the modest fashion sphere.

@zeinab.harake: Uplifting content on self-care, beauty routines, and body positivity.

Food and Cooking:

@muslimahchef: Delicious halal recipes and cooking tips for busy individuals.

@healthyhalalmama: Healthy and family-friendly halal food inspiration.

@chef.salma: Creative and modern takes on traditional halal dishes.

@thehalalfoodie: Discover new halal restaurants and cuisines around the world.

@muslimvegan: Plant-based halal recipes and insights on sustainable living.

Business and Entrepreneurship:

@muslimgirlboss: Inspiring stories and resources for Muslim women entrepreneurs.

@themuslimahceo: Empowering women to build successful halal businesses.

@muslimfinance: Financial literacy tips and resources tailored for Muslim communities.

@digitalmuslimah: Practical advice on navigating the digital world as a Muslim woman.

@halaltravelgirl: Inspiration and resources for Muslim women seeking travel adventures.

Remember, this is just a small selection, and many other amazing Muslim women influencers are out there! Explore hashtags like #muslimwomen, #hijabifashion, #muslimgirlboss, and discover inspiring accounts that resonate with your interests.

Using LinkedIn to promote your business

Here's a step-by-step guide:

Create a Company Page:

Set up a LinkedIn Company Page. This acts as your business's LinkedIn profile.

Include a detailed description of your business, industry, and website link.

Optimize Your Profile:

Use relevant keywords for your industry to improve searchability.

Keep information up-to-date and professional.

Publish Engaging Content:

Regularly post updates, articles, and insights related to your industry.

Share success stories, case studies, and testimonials.

Use Rich Media:

Incorporate images and videos in your posts to boost engagement.

Create infographics or short clips that explain your products or services.

Leverage LinkedIn Articles:

Publish in-depth articles directly on LinkedIn. This positions you as an industry thought leader.

Network Actively:

Connect with industry professionals, potential clients, and partners.

Engage with others 'posts by commenting and sharing.

Join and Participate in Groups:

Join LinkedIn groups relevant to your industry.

Actively participate in discussions and offer valuable insights.

Employee Advocacy:

Encourage your employees to create and maintain professional LinkedIn profiles.

Have them share your company's content to broaden reach.

Use LinkedIn Ads:

Consider using LinkedIn's advertising tools to reach a wider audience.

Target your ads based on job title, industry, company size, etc.

Collect and Showcase Recommendations:

Request recommendations from satisfied clients or partners.

Display these on your company page to build credibility.

LinkedIn Analytics:

Utilize LinkedIn Analytics to understand the impact of your content.

Adjust your strategy based on these insights.

Host a LinkedIn Live Session:

Use LinkedIn Live to host webinars, Q&A sessions, or product demonstrations.

Interact with your audience in real-time.

Regular Updates:

Keep your followers informed about company news, product launches, and events.

Personal Branding:

Strengthen your personal brand as a leader or founder.

Your personal professional network can significantly impact your business's visibility.

Customer Engagement:

Promptly respond to comments and messages.

Foster a community around your brand.

By consistently engaging with your audience and offering valuable content, you can effectively use LinkedIn not just to promote your business but also to establish yourself as a thought leader in your industry.

List of some groups in LinkedIn:

General:

Muslim Business Network (MBN): https://www.linkedin.com/company/muslim-community-network

Muslim Professionals Network (MPN): http://www.camp-online.org/

Muslim Women Professionals (MWP): https://www.muslimwomenprofessionals.org/

Muslim Council of Professionals (MCP): https://mcb.org.uk/

Muslim Entrepreneurs & Professionals (MEP): https://arabian-mep.com/

Finance and Investment:

Islamic Finance Group (IFG): https://uk.linkedin.com/company/islamicfinanceguru

Muslim Investor Network (MIN): http://www.islamicinvestmentnetwork.com/

Tech and Innovation:

Muslim Startup Network (MSN): https://startup-muslim.fr/connexion/

Muslim Innovation Network (MIN): https://mcnny.org/

Industry Specific:

Muslim Lawyers Network (MLN): http://www.muslimlegalnetworknsw.com/

Additional Resources:

LinkedIn Group Search: Use keywords like "Muslim business," "Islamic finance," "Muslim entrepreneurs," etc.

LinkedIn Events: Attend online or offline events hosted by Muslim business groups.

LinkedIn Pulse: Follow articles and posts from influential voices in the Muslim professional community.

Please note that not all groups have active LinkedIn presences, but the links provided are the most relevant I could find.

Creating Engaging Facebook, Instagram, and LinkedIn Groups:

Building a strong online community through Facebook, Instagram, and LinkedIn groups can be a powerful tool for Muslim women entrepreneurs.

Here's a breakdown of how to create and manage successful groups on each platform:

Facebook Groups:

1. Set Up:

- Go to your Facebook profile and click "Create Group".
- Choose a relevant and catchy name.
- Select a privacy setting (Public, Private, or Hidden).
- Write a clear and engaging group description outlining your purpose and target audience.
- Set ground rules and community guidelines.
- Choose an eye-catching cover photo and group icon.

2. Promote and Invite Members:

- Share your group on your personal Facebook profile and other relevant pages.
- Run targeted Facebook ads to reach potential members.
- Collaborate with other Facebook groups or pages for cross-promotion.
- Share valuable content regularly to keep members engaged.
- Organize live events, Q&A sessions, and discussions.

- Encourage members to invite their friends and colleagues.

Instagram Groups:

1. Enable Group Chat:
- Go to your Instagram profile and tap the "+" icon.
- Select "Chat" and click "Create Group".
- Add members and name your group.
- Set group rules and manage notifications.

2. Promote and Engage Members:
- Share your group in your Instagram stories and bio.
- Run Instagram ads targeting your ideal audience.
- Use relevant hashtags to increase discoverability.
- Create engaging polls, quizzes, and Q&A sessions.
- Host live video sessions and AMAs.
- Share exclusive content and behind-the-scenes glimpses.
- Feature user-generated content and stories.

LinkedIn Groups:

1. Create and Customize:
- Go to your LinkedIn profile and click "Work".
- Select "Groups" and click "Create Group".

- Choose a relevant name, description, and category.
- Customize the group settings and visibility.
- Upload a logo and cover photo.

2. Grow and Engage Members:

- Share your group on your LinkedIn profile and relevant networks.
- Reach out to potential members directly and invite them to join.
- Organize industry-specific discussions and webinars.
- Share valuable articles, resources, and job opportunities.
- Run polls and surveys to gauge members' interests.
- Host networking events and Q&A sessions.
- Recognize and reward active members.

Additional Tips:

- Be clear about your group's purpose and target audience.
- Post consistently and provide valuable content.
- Engage with your members and respond to their questions and comments.
- Foster a safe and respectful environment for all members.
- Adapt your strategies based on member feedback and engagement data.

- Collaborate with other groups and communities for wider reach.

By following these steps and tailoring your approach to each platform, you can create thriving Facebook, Instagram, and LinkedIn groups that support your business goals and empower your Muslim women entrepreneur community

Power of Unity

Sisters, as we stand poised at the precipice of our entrepreneurial journeys, let the blessed words of Prophet Muhammad (peace be upon him) echo in our hearts: "The believers are like a single body; if one part is in pain, the whole body feels its pain." These verses, woven with threads of wisdom and compassion, illuminate the path ahead, revealing the profound strength that lies not in solitary pursuit, but in the tapestry of unity and collaboration.

Just as the Prophet (peace be upon him) navigated the turbulent seas of his time, forging alliances and weaving treaties with other tribes, we too can embrace the winds of cooperation. Let us not mistake competition for the sole engine of progress. Instead, let us see it as a spark, igniting the fire of innovation and pushing us to hone our skills, refine our offerings, and strive for excellence. But that fire, sisters, burns brightest when fueled by the shared warmth of collaboration.

Imagine, sisters, a bustling marketplace where Muslim women, diverse in talents and passions, stand shoulder to shoulder. The perfumer, her fingers stained with the essence of jasmine, shares her knowledge with the weaver, whose loom sings with vibrant stories. The tech whiz, her mind a constellation of code, joins hands with the marketing guru, whose words paint captivating landscapes. The lawyer, a shield against injustice, walks alongside the social worker, her heart a beacon of hope. In this kaleidoscope of collaboration, each sister's strengths amplify the other's, creating a symphony of success that resonates far beyond individual triumphs.

Think of the knowledge we can glean from one another, sisters! The seasoned businesswoman can mentor the budding entrepreneur, her wisdom a compass guiding her through the uncharted waters of the market. The graphic designer can lend her creative eye to the struggling writer, her visuals giving voice to unspoken stories. The digital strategist can share her online prowess with the brick-and-mortar veteran, bridging the gap between tradition and innovation. In this exchange of knowledge, we become not just competitors, but co-creators, weaving a tapestry of success that bears the imprint of each and every sister.

But our collaboration, sisters, transcends the confines of mere business. It is a woven cloak of support, shielding us from the storms that inevitably arise. The struggling sister finds solace in the arms of a fellow entrepreneur, her empathy a balm on wounded ambition. The sister facing legal hurdles finds her voice amplified by the lawyer's expertise, her justice a collective victory. The sister burdened by societal expectations finds strength in the whispers of encouragement, her resilience fueled by the unwavering belief of her sisters.

So, sisters, as we embark on this journey of entrepreneurship, let us not forget the Prophet's (peace be upon him) words. Let them be our guiding light, reminding us that we are not islands in a vast ocean, but threads in a vibrant tapestry. Let us weave our strengths together, share our knowledge, and support each other through the triumphs and tribulations. For in unity, sisters, lies not just our success, but the potential to change the world, one collaborative thread at a time.

May the blessings of Allah be upon our endeavors, may He guide our steps, and may our sisterhood be the wind that propels us to heights unimaginable. Ameen.

Tips:

Identifying Like-minded Partners:

- Seek out sisters in online communities like Muslimapreneurs Network, Muslim Businesswomen's Network, or local Facebook groups specifically for Muslim women entrepreneurs. This opens doors to networking opportunities and potential partnerships.

- Connect with complementary businesses. Consider partnering with a graphic designer like Hana Design Studio, a web developer like UmmahTech, or a social media manager from Halal Social Media

Marketing to create a comprehensive brand image. This allows you to leverage each other's expertise and strengthen your online presence.

- Attend industry events like the Islamic Economy Forum, Global Islamic Finance Summit, or Halal Expo.These events offer valuable opportunities to network with potential collaborators, learn from industry leaders, and gain insights into the latest trends.

Exploring Cross-promotional Opportunities:

- Utilize social media scheduling tools like Hootsuite or Buffer to schedule cross-promotions in advance. This ensures consistent engagement and avoids overwhelming your audience with simultaneous posts.

- Write guest blog posts on each other's websites or blogs. Share your expertise in areas like halal fashion with a fellow clothing brand or discuss Islamic finance tips on a financial advisor's website, expanding your reach and audience base.

- Host Instagram takeovers. Allow a fellow entrepreneur like Mariam from "Mariam's Modest Fashion" to take over your Instagram story for a day, introducing your audience to her brand and vice versa. This provides a fresh perspective and increases engagement.

Hosting Joint Events and Webinars:

- Organize online workshops. Utilize video conferencing platforms like Zoom or Google Meet to host workshops on topics relevant to your industry, like personal branding for entrepreneurs with expert Sarah from "Sara's Branding Academy". This provides valuable learning experiences for your audience and builds your reputation as an industry leader.

- Partner with local organizations. Host networking events at community centers, mosques, or co-working spaces like "The Muslimah Hub" to connect with potential customers and collaborators. This builds awareness and fosters community support for your businesses.

- Co-host webinars. Combine your expertise and host webinars on topics like Islamic marketing with Amina from "Amina's Islamic Marketing Agency" or halal business practices with Omar from "Omar's Halal Consulting", offering diverse perspectives and attracting a wider audience. This strengthens your credibility and expands your reach.

Amplifying Each Other's Voices:

- Leave positive reviews on each other's websites, Google My Business listings, or social media pages. This demonstrates your support and encourages potential customers to explore their businesses.

- Celebrate your fellow sisters' achievements on your platforms, inspiring and motivating others. Share their success stories on your website, social media, or even include them in a blog post titled "Inspirational Muslim Women Entrepreneurs". This showcases the positive impact of your community and encourages collaboration.

- Collaborate on social media campaigns. Create a hashtag campaign together like #EmpoweringMuslimWomen and encourage your followers to participate, promoting both your brands and raising awareness about your collective mission. This amplifies your message and strengthens your collective impact.

Creating Joint Ventures:

- Co-develop products. Combine your skills and expertise to create a new product or service that caters to your combined audience. Consider co-creating a line of Islamic clothing with a modest fashion designer or developing an app for Muslim children with a software developer. This leverages your individual strengths and creates an offering that appeals to a wider audience.

- Offer bundles and deals. Partner with complementary businesses like a local bakery to offer a special Ramadan bundle that includes your handcrafted hijabs and their delicious pastries, attracting new customers and increasing sales for both businesses. This creates a win-win situation and provides value to your customers.

- Participate in joint marketing initiatives. Share marketing costs and resources to launch joint marketing campaigns, maximizing your reach and impact. Partner with a digital marketing agency like "Crescent Digital" to develop a comprehensive campaign targeting your ideal customers. This optimizes your marketing budget and leverages the agency's expertise.

Forming Mentorship and Support Networks:

- Join online mentoring programs. Platforms like Muslimah Mentorship or MPowered Women connect aspiring entrepreneurs with experienced mentors like Khadija from "Khadija's Business Coaching" who can offer valuable guidance and support. This provides access to expertise and experience that you may not have otherwise.

- Connect with other entrepreneurs in your community. Attend local networking events or join online communities to connect with other entrepreneurs who can offer support, advice, and encouragement. This provides a sense of community and belonging that can be invaluable.

- Create your own mentorship program. If you have the experience and expertise, consider offering mentorship to other aspiring entrepreneurs. This is a great way to give back to your community and share your knowledge and wisdom with others.

Participating in Industry Associations and Events:

- Join professional organizations. Organizations like the Islamic Chamber of Commerce and Industry or the Muslim Business Council offer networking opportunities, educational resources, and advocacy on behalf of Muslim businesses. This provides access to industry knowledge and resources that can help you grow your business.

- Attend industry events. Events like the Islamic Economy Summit or the Global Islamic Finance Forum offer valuable opportunities to network with other professionals, learn about the latest trends, and gain insights into the industry landscape. This provides exposure to new opportunities and helps you stay ahead of the curve.

Utilizing Online Collaboration Tools:

- Use project management software. Tools like Asana or Trello can help you track progress, assign tasks, and collaborate effectively on joint projects. This ensures that everyone is on the same page and helps you avoid delays or miscommunication.

- Use video conferencing tools. Tools like Zoom or Google Meet can help you connect with other collaborators in real time, regardless of their location. This facilitates communication and collaboration and can help you build stronger relationships.

- Use cloud-based storage. Tools like Dropbox or Google Drive can help you share files and collaborate on documents easily. This streamlines the collaboration process and helps you save time and resources.

- I will share a list of important resources to use with your business*

Celebrating Diversity and Inclusion:

- Be open to working with people from different backgrounds. Diversity of thought and experience can lead to new ideas and innovation.

- Be respectful of different cultures, religions and perspectives. Remember that everyone has something to offer, and be willing to learn from others.

- Create a welcoming and inclusive environment. Make sure everyone feels comfortable and valued, regardless of their background.

Collaboration is a powerful tool that can help Muslim women entrepreneurs grow their businesses, build their networks, and empower one another. By following the strategies outlined in this guide, you can leverage the power of collaboration to achieve your business goals and make a positive impact on the world.

Here are some additional tips for collaborating effectively with other Muslim women entrepreneurs:

- Be clear about your expectations and goals. Before you begin collaborating with someone, make sure you are on the same page about what you want to achieve.

- Communicate regularly. Keep in touch with your collaborators throughout the collaboration process, and be open to feedback and suggestions.

- Be flexible and willing to compromise. Things don't always go according to plan, so be prepared to adapt and make changes as needed.

- Celebrate your successes together. When you achieve a goal, take the time to celebrate your success with your collaborators. This will help to build camaraderie and strengthen your relationship.

By following these tips, you can build strong and lasting relationships with other Muslim women entrepreneurs, cr

Platform Selection

Choosing the right platform to sell your services and products, share your knowledge, or build your online presence is crucial for success in today's digital landscape. With a plethora of options available, understanding your target audience and tailoring your approach to each platform is key to reaching your ideal customers, readers, or students. This section provides a comprehensive overview of popular platforms to consider, along with strategies for tailoring your content and approach to each one:

Let's explore some of the platforms that can become your launchpad:

E-commerce Platforms:

Shopify: https://www.shopify.com/ (A leading platform with powerful built-in tools, themes, and customization options, ideal for established businesses with a wider range of products.)

Etsy: https://www.etsy.com/ (A popular platform for handcrafted and vintage items, perfect for showcasing unique products from Muslim artisans.)

Amazon: https://www.amazon.com/ (A global marketplace with vast reach and fulfillment services, ideal for businesses with established brands and large product catalogs.)

Ebay: https://www.ebay.com/ (Another global marketplace with a focus on individual sellers, offering auction and fixed-price listing options.)

Souq:* (A leading platform in the Middle East and North Africa, ideal for reaching customers in the region.)

*Souq may not be an active anymore, its legacy holds valuable lessons for aspiring Muslim entrepreneurs. Studying its story can provide insights into navigating the e-commerce landscape, even as new platforms emerge.

Think of it as a historical case study, sisters. We can learn from Souq's successes, like its focus on the Middle East and North African market, and its dedication to building a community around its sellers. We can also learn from its challenges, like adapting to changing consumer trends and keeping up with competitive forces.

Remember, knowledge is power, even if it comes from closed chapters. By understanding Souq's journey, we can better prepare for our own ventures. The lessons learned can be applied to other platforms, helping us navigate the ever-evolving world of online commerce.

So, while Souq may be closed, its story remains open to us. Let's take inspiration from its triumphs and learn from its stumbles, sisters. Together, we can build our own success stories, ones that stand tall in the ever-changing landscape of e-commerce. May the spirit of innovation and collaboration guide us!

Here's the Wikipedia link to Souq for those who want to delve deeper:

https://en.wikipedia.org/wiki/Souq_%28company %29)

Social Commerce Platforms:

Facebook   Marketplace: https://www.facebook.com/marketplace (A built-in marketplace within Facebook, allowing users to buy and sell locally, perfect for reaching local customers and building community around your brand.)

Instagram   Shopping: https://www.instagram.com/shop/?hl=en (Enables businesses to sell directly through their profiles and stories, ideal for visually appealing products and engaging with a young audience.)

TikTok Shop: https://shop.tiktok.com/ (A rapidly growing platform for short-form video content with integrated shopping features, suitable for brands with a young target audience.)

Service-based Platforms:

Maximize Your Productivity with Fiverr: Budget-Friendly Solutions for Busy Muslim Entrepreneurs

Sisters, in our pursuit of success, efficiency is key. While time is precious, resources can be limited. Enter Fiverr, a platform brimming with skilled freelancers ready to tackle your tasks at surprisingly affordable rates.

Website copywriting: Captivating product descriptions and engaging blog posts for under $5.

Social media management: Scheduled posts, engaging captions, and community management for as low as $10.

Graphic design: Eye-catching logos, social media graphics, and website banners starting at $5.

Data entry: Organize your spreadsheets and customer lists for a mere $5.

Basic video editing: Create video intros and promos for less than $10.

Fiverr's micro-services empower you to:

Delegate tasks: Free up your time to focus on core business activities.

Access specialized skills: Tap into a diverse talent pool without incurring significant costs.

Experiment and iterate: Test new ideas and refine your approach without breaking the bank.

Embrace Fiverr's budget-friendly:

Reduce operational costs: Invest in specific tasks without the overhead of full-time employees.

Empower other Muslim entrepreneurs: Support fellow sisters by utilizing their skills and talents.

Remember, sisters, every dollar saved is a dollar invested in your success. Fiverr is not just about affordability, it's about unlocking your full potential. So, explore Fiverr's micro-magic today and watch your business soar.

May your entrepreneurial journey be blessed with productivity, efficiency, and unwavering sisterhood. Ameen!

Fiverr: https://www.fiverr.com/ (Another platform for freelance services, offering a range of project-based and hourly gigs.)

Similar to Fiverr:

Upwork: https://www.upwork.com/ (A platform for freelancers and agencies to connect with clients for various services, from design and marketing to writing and translation.)

Guru: https://www.guru.com/ (A platform for finding and hiring freelance professionals, offering a range of services related to business, IT, and design.)

Content Creation and Education Platforms:

KDP (Kindle Direct Publishing): https://kdp.amazon.com/ (Allows authors to self-publish ebooks and paperbacks and make them available for sale on Amazon, ideal for sharing your knowledge and expertise in a structured format.)

Coursera: https://www.coursera.org/ (A platform for online courses offered by universities and other institutions, suitable for building professional learning experiences.)

Udemy: https://www.udemy.com/ (A platform for online courses offered by individuals and organizations, perfect for sharing your expertise and skills with a wider audience.)

These are just a few stepping stones on your entrepreneurial path, sisters. Remember, the key is to choose platforms that align with your strengths, target audience, and product offerings. But most importantly, remember the power of collaboration. Seek out fellow Muslim entrepreneurs, share your experiences and knowledge, and build a supportive network that uplifts and empowers you. As you weave your threads of success together, may your journey be blessed with prosperity, guidance, and the unwavering spirit of sisterhood. Ameen.

May Allah guide your steps and grant you barakah in all your endeavors. Go forth, sisters, and change the world!

What is SEO?

SEO (Search Engine Optimization): It's like teaching Google or other search engines about your website so it can recommend it to people who are looking for information you have.

SEO, or Search Engine Optimization, is crucial for your business because it's the key to visibility in the digital world. Just imagine your website as a hidden gem in a vast desert – without SEO, it's almost impossible for potential customers to find you. Here's why SEO is so important:

Things to keep in mind for a good SEO

Keyword Research

- Tools: These are like special magnifying glasses that help you find the right words people are using on Google.
- Long-Tail Keywords: These are longer phrases that are very specific and easier to rank for.
- Search Intent: Understanding why people are searching for those words.

Content

- Quality Content: This means creating information that is helpful, interesting, and what your audience wants to know.

- Consistency: Regularly adding new and interesting things to your website.
- Multimedia: Including pictures, videos, and graphics to make your website more engaging.

Page Optimization

- Title Tags: These are the titles of your web pages that you see in Google search results.
- Headings (H1, H2, etc.): These are like chapter titles in a book, helping to organize your content.
- Alt Text for Images: Describing your pictures to Google and people who can't see them.
- Building Backlinks: Getting other reputable websites to link to your website.
- Social Media Engagement: Talking and interacting with people on social media platforms.
- Influencer Outreach: Connecting with popular people on social media to promote your website.

Technical SEO Essentials

- Secure and Accessible Website: Making sure your website is safe and can be easily visited.
- XML Sitemap: A map that helps Google find all the pages of your website.

- Robots.txt: A guide for Google, telling it what parts of your website it should and shouldn't look at.

Measuring SEO Success

- Google Analytics: A tool to see how many people visit your website and what they do there.

- Rank Tracking: Watching how high your website appears in Google over time.

- Conversion Rate: Checking how often visitors do what you want them to do (like buying something).

SEO Trends and Algorithm Updates

- Staying Informed: Keeping up with changes in how Google ranks websites.

- Adapting Strategies: Changing your strategies based on new trends and rules.

Local SEO

- Google My Business: A Google profile for your local business so people can find you easily.

- Local Keywords: Words that include locations to attract local customers.

- Local Backlinks: Links from local businesses or websites.

E-commerce SEO

- Product Descriptions: Writing unique and detailed descriptions for the products on your online store.

- Structured Data Markup: This is like adding labels to your content so Google understands it better and can show it in special ways in search results.

Mobile SEO

- Responsive Design: Making sure your website changes its layout to look good on any device.

- Mobile Speed: Making your website load quickly on mobile devices.

Conclusion

SEO is like making your website a friendly and informative place that Google wants to recommend to people. It involves making your content great, ensuring your website works well technically, and getting other people and websites to talk about you. By doing this, you help your website appear higher in Google's search results, getting more people to visit your site.

Strategically Utilize Paid Advertising:

Consider investing in targeted social media advertising campaigns to significantly increase your reach and attract potential customers actively searching for products or services like yours. Utilize platform-specific tools to define your ideal customer profile and create targeted campaigns that resonate deeply with their needs and interests.

Let us begin by laying the foundation:

Creating your accounts:

Google Ads

- Create a Google Ads Account:
- Visit the Google Ads website.
- Click on "Start now".
- Sign in with your Google account or create a new one.
- Set Your Campaign Goal:
- Choose your main advertising goal: getting more calls, website visits, or physical store visits.
- Select the Campaign Type:

- Choose where you want your ads to appear (e.g., on Google Search, YouTube).
- Define Your Audience and Budget:
- Select geographical locations where you want to advertise.
- Set your daily budget.
- Create Your Ads:
- Write your ad copy, keeping it relevant and engaging.
- Add keywords that are relevant to your product or service.
- Launch and Monitor:
- Once everything is set, launch your campaign.
- Regularly monitor performance and adjust as needed.

Facebook Ads

- Create a Facebook Business Page:
- You need a business page to run ads.
- Set Up Facebook Ads Manager:
- Access Ads Manager through your Facebook account.

- Provide business and payment information.
- Choose Your Objective:
- Select what you want to achieve, like brand awareness, traffic, or sales.
- Target Your Audience:
- Define your audience based on demographics, interests, and behaviors.
- Set Budget and Schedule:
- Decide on a daily or lifetime budget.
- Schedule your ad's run time.
- Design Your Ad:
- Use high-quality images or videos.
- Write compelling ad copy.
- Launch and Monitor:
- Review and launch your campaign.
- Regularly check performance metrics.

Etsy Ads

- Open an Etsy Shop:
- You need an active shop to use Etsy Ads.
- Access Etsy Ads:
- Go to your Shop Manager and select "Advertising".
- Set Your Budget:

- Decide on the amount you're willing to spend daily.
- Select Listings to Advertise:
- You can let Etsy choose or select listings manually.
- Review and Launch:
- Review your settings and start your campaign.

Amazon Ads

- Create an Amazon Seller Account:
- Go to Amazon Seller Central and sign up.
- Choose Your Ad Type:
- Select between Sponsored Products, Sponsored Brands, and more.
- Set Your Campaign:
- Define campaign name, duration, and budget.
- Target Your Ads:
- Choose keywords or products to target.
- Create Your Ad:
- Add relevant product details and images.
- Launch and Monitor:
- Start your campaign and keep an eye on its performance.

LinkedIn Ads

- Create a LinkedIn Campaign Manager Account:
- Go to LinkedIn Campaign Manager and sign in with your LinkedIn account.
- Set up an account by entering your business details.
- Choose Your Objective:
- Select from options like brand awareness, lead generation, or engagement.
- Target Your Audience:
- Use criteria like job title, company size, industry, etc., for precise targeting.
- Set Your Budget and Schedule:
- Decide on a daily budget, bid type, and the duration of the campaign.
- Create Your Ad:
- Choose from various ad formats (sponsored content, InMail, text ads).
- Design your ad with compelling copy and visuals.
- Launch and Monitor:
- Start your campaign and use LinkedIn Analytics to track performance.

Twitter (X) Ads

- Set Up a Twitter Ads Account:
- Use your Twitter account to access Twitter Ads.
- Add your payment information.
- Define Your Campaign Objective:
- Options include website clicks, app installs, followers, etc.
- Target Your Audience:
- Segment your audience based on interests, demographics, behavior, etc.
- Choose Your Budget:
- Set a total budget and choose how much to bid per interaction.
- Design Your Ad:
- Use engaging visuals and concise, clear messaging.
- Launch and Monitor:
- Go live with your campaign and monitor using Twitter's analytics tools.

Instagram Ads

- Have a Facebook Page and Ad Account:
- Instagram ads are managed through Facebook's platform.
- Link Instagram to Your Facebook Page:
- Connect your Instagram account to your Facebook page.

- Create Your Campaign in Facebook Ads Manager:
- Choose your objective, audience, budget, and schedule.
- Design Your Ad:
- Use high-quality visuals and engaging captions.
- Choose ad placement to include Instagram.
- Launch and Monitor:
- Publish your ad and track performance through Facebook Ads Manager.

Pinterest Ads

- Create a Pinterest Business Account:
- Sign up for a business account or convert your existing account.
- Set Up Ad Campaign:
- Go to Ads Manager and choose your campaign goal.
- Target Your Audience:

- Define your audience based on interests, demographics, and keywords.
- Set Budget and Schedule:
- Decide on your daily or lifetime budget and campaign duration.
- Choose Your Pins for Promotion:
- Select existing Pins to promote, ensuring they are high quality and relevant.
- Launch and Monitor:
- Start your campaign and use Pinterest Analytics for tracking.

TikTok Ads

- Create a TikTok Ads Account:
- Sign up for a TikTok Ads account.
- Set Up Your Campaign:
- Choose an objective like traffic, app installs, or conversions.
- Define Your Audience:
- Segment your audience based on demographics, interests, and behaviors.
- Budget and Bidding:
- Set your budget and bid strategy.
- Create Your Ad:
- Use engaging and creative video content tailored for TikTok's audience.

- Launch and Monitor:
- Publish your campaign and monitor performance using TikTok's analytics.

General Tips for All Platforms:

- Consistent Branding: Ensure your ads align with your brand voice and image.

- Engaging Content: Use high-quality visuals and compelling copy.

- Optimize for Mobile: Most social media users access platforms via mobile devices.

- Test and Learn: Experiment with different ad formats and content to see what works best.

- Track and Analyze: Regularly review analytics to understand ad performance and ROI.

- Understand Your Audience: Tailor your ads to the interests and behaviors of your target demographic.

- A/B Testing: Regularly test different ad versions to see what works best.

- Analytics: Use platform-specific analytics tools to monitor performance and ROI.
- Adapt and Optimize: Continuously refine your campaigns based on performance data.

Remember, success in advertising is a journey, not a destination. By consistently learning, adapting, and optimizing your campaigns, you can harness the power of online advertising to reach new audiences, boost your brand awareness,and achieve your business goals. May our ads be not just marketing messages, but bridges that connect us to our audiences, inspire action, and leave a lasting impact.

Analyze and Adapt for Continuous Growth

Data is your friend. Regularly track your social media performance and analyze key metrics to understand what content resonates with your audience and what areas require improvement. Adapt your strategies based on your findings and continuously strive to refine your online presence for optimal engagement and growth.

Embrace Social Commerce Features:

Streamline the customer journey and leverage built-in features like Instagram Shops and Facebook Marketplace to sell your products directly through your social media platforms. This user-friendly approach provides convenient access for your audience to discover your offerings, complete their purchases, and become loyal customers.

Be Authentic and Consistent:

Remember, your online presence is an extension of your unique personality and values. Remain true to your core beliefs,be consistent in your communication and brand messaging, and let your genuine passion shine through. This builds trust with your audience, establishes a strong brand identity, and lays the foundation for long-term success.

Sisters, by embracing these comprehensive strategies and harnessing the power of social media and online platforms, you can embark on a fulfilling entrepreneurial journey, connect with your target audience, and build a thriving business that empowers your community and resonates with your values. Remember, the digital world is your canvas. Paint your unique vision, amplify your voice, and conquer the entrepreneurial realm with confidence and faith.

Utilize social media and online platforms: Connect with potential customers and build your brand presence through platforms like Facebook, Instagram, and YouTube. Create engaging content that resonates with both Muslim and non-Muslim audiences.

Balancing Entrepreneurship with Family and Religious Obligations

Dear Sisters, In our journey as entrepreneurs, balancing our professional ambitions with the deep-rooted values of family and religious obligations can be a fulfilling yet challenging endeavor. It is a path of commitment, understanding, and harmony, where every role we undertake is a testament to our strength and faith.

When it comes to entrepreneurship, let us embrace it with passion and diligence. Remember, our work is not just a means to an end but a reflection of our capabilities and our contribution to the community. However, this pursuit should never overshadow the importance of our families. The warmth and support of a family create a foundation upon which we can build our dreams and aspirations. Cherish these moments, for they are precious and irreplaceable.

Simultaneously, our religious duties hold a sacred place in our lives. These practices are not just rituals but the essence of our existence, guiding us through the ebb and flow of life. They remind us of the bigger picture, our values, and our connection to the Almighty. Balancing our work with these spiritual responsibilities requires mindfulness and planning. Set aside specific times for prayer and reflection, ensuring they are a priority in your daily schedule.

Honoring our husbands is a partnership of mutual respect and love. It's about understanding and supporting each other's dreams, aspirations, and responsibilities. In your entrepreneurial journey, involve your husband, share your challenges and successes, and seek his counsel. This journey, when shared, strengthens the bond and brings a deeper understanding and appreciation for each other's roles.

Similarly, our parents deserve our utmost respect and care. They have shaped us into who we are. As entrepreneurs, we might find ourselves engulfed in our work, but let's not forget the sacrifices and love our parents have bestowed upon us. Make time for them, involve them in your life, and seek their blessings and advice. Their wisdom is invaluable, and their happiness brings divine contentment.

Lastly, in all these roles, be kind to yourself. Understand that perfection is not the goal; it's about effort, growth, and balance. There will be days when things don't go as planned, when the balance seems off. In those moments, lean on your faith, your family, and remember why you started. Your journey is unique and beautiful, filled with lessons and blessings.

May your path be enlightened with wisdom, patience, and prosperity, and may you find joy and fulfillment in each role you cherish.

Inspiring Success Stories

Sahar Hashemi: A Beacon of Innovation in the Business World

Sahar Hashemi is a name synonymous with entrepreneurial spirit and innovation. A British businesswoman with a captivating story, she has carved her niche in the food and beverage industry, leaving an indelible mark with her unique perspectives and impactful ventures.

Born in 1967, Sahar's journey began with a legal career, but her entrepreneurial spirit soon nudged her towards a different path. In 1995, she co-founded Coffee Republic, the UK's first US-style coffee bar chain. This bold move marked a turning point in the British coffee culture, introducing a vibrant café experience that resonated with the public. Coffee Republic quickly became a household name, with its stylish outlets and diverse coffee blends catering to a growing demand for quality coffee experiences. Sahar's vision and leadership proved instrumental in the company's success, solidifying her position as a force to be reckoned with in the industry.

But Sahar's ambitions didn't stop there. In 2007, she co-founded Skinny Candy, a confectionery brand focused on creating healthy and delicious treats. Recognizing the growing awareness of health and wellness, Skinny Candy offered a unique alternative to conventional sugary snacks. The brand quickly gained popularity, with its innovative sugar-free and low-calorie offerings catering to a conscious consumer base. This venture further cemented Sahar's reputation as a pioneer,constantly pushing boundaries and challenging the status quo in the food and beverage landscape.

Throughout her career, Sahar has consistently demonstrated exceptional business acumen, strategic thinking, and a keen eye for emerging trends. Her ability to identify and capitalize on untapped markets has fueled her success, making her a role model for aspiring entrepreneurs and business leaders alike.

Beyond her entrepreneurial endeavors, Sahar has actively engaged in various initiatives promoting innovation and female empowerment. She has served as a speaker ambassador for the Prince's Trust and a lecturer at the London Business School Entrepreneurship program. Her passion for supporting and inspiring others extends beyond the boardroom,making her a true advocate for positive change in the business world.

Sahar's contributions to the food and beverage industry have been recognized by numerous awards and accolades. She was named one of the "20 most powerful women in the UK" by Director magazine and awarded an OBE (Officer of the Order of the British Empire) for her services to business.

However, Sahar's true legacy lies beyond awards and recognition. It resides in her unwavering commitment to innovation,her dedication to empowering others, and her unwavering belief in the power of entrepreneurship to create positive change. For Sahar Hashemi is not just a successful businesswoman; she is a visionary leader, a trailblazer, and an inspiration to aspiring entrepreneurs across the globe.

As Sahar continues to delve into new ventures and explore uncharted territories, one thing remains certain: her impact on the business world will continue to resonate for years to come. She is a true testament to the power of innovation,resilience, and a spirit that dares to dream big and make a difference.

Her story serves as a beacon of hope and inspiration, encouraging aspiring entrepreneurs to forge their own paths,embrace challenges, and leave their own indelible mark on the world. The journey of Sahar Hashemi is far from over, and one can only anticipate with excitement the next innovative chapter that unfolds in her remarkable and inspiring story.

Raja Easa Al Gurg: A Visionary Leader Shaping the Future

A name synonymous with success, innovation, and unwavering passion, Raja Easa Al Gurg is a force to be reckoned with in the world of business and philanthropy. A trailblazer in the Middle East, she stands as a testament to the power of resilience, determination, and unwavering commitment to one's values.

Born into a prominent Emirati family, Raja's journey began in the vibrant city of Dubai. Surrounded by the spirit of entrepreneurship and a deep-rooted cultural heritage, she embarked on her own path, fueled by an insatiable thirst for knowledge and a desire to make a positive impact on her community.

Her education laid the foundation for her remarkable achievements. Armed with a degree from Kuwait University, she entered the world of business, ready to contribute her talents and vision to the ever-evolving landscape of Dubai.

Raja's leadership style is marked by a unique blend of strategic thinking, unwavering integrity, and a deep understanding of the human spirit. From her early days at the Easa Saleh Al Gurg Group, a family-owned conglomerate, she has played a pivotal role in its expansion and diversification, overseeing its transformation into a global powerhouse spanning across diverse sectors.

But her vision extended far beyond the realm of profit. Raja is a champion of social responsibility and sustainable development, actively promoting education, healthcare initiatives, and fostering a spirit of community engagement.

In a region where women's roles are often perceived in a narrow light, Raja stands tall as an inspiring example of what Muslim women can achieve. She shatters stereotypes, dismantling barriers, and paving the way for future generations to dream and reach for the stars.

Her commitment to empowering women is evident through her numerous initiatives, including the founding of the Dubai Business Women Council, a platform designed to equip women with the necessary skills and resources to navigate the complexities of the business world.

Raja's dedication to her community extends beyond the boardroom. She is a renowned philanthropist, actively supporting causes close to her heart, such as education, healthcare, and environmental sustainability. Her unwavering belief in the power of giving back has touched countless lives, leaving a lasting impact on the fabric of society.

Raja's influence transcends geographical boundaries. Recognized as one of the most influential women in the Arab world,she is a sought-after speaker and advisor, sharing her wisdom and experience with global audiences. She actively participates in international forums, advocating for entrepreneurship, cultural exchange, and promoting a deeper understanding of the Arab world.

Throughout her remarkable journey, Raja has faced challenges and adversities with grace and fortitude. Her indomitable spirit and unwavering faith have served as her compass, guiding her through turbulent times and propelling her towards even greater heights.

Today, Raja Easa Al Gurg stands as a beacon of hope and inspiration for aspiring entrepreneurs, particularly women,across the globe. Her story is a testament to the limitless potential that lies within each of us, a testament to the power of perseverance, and a reminder that success is not just about achieving goals, but about the positive impact we leave on the world around us.

As Raja continues her remarkable journey, one thing remains certain: her legacy will endure, inspiring generations to come to embrace their dreams, challenge the status quo, and strive for a better tomorrow.

Bayan Mahmoud Al-Zahran: A Beacon of Inspiration for Muslim Women

Bayan Mahmoud Al-Zahran is more than just a name. It represents a symbol of hope, resilience, and determination for countless women across the globe. As one of the first female lawyers in Saudi Arabia, she has paved the way for a generation of women to dream bigger and reach for seemingly impossible goals. Her journey is a testament to the power of individual action and the transformative impact it can have on society as a whole.

Born in 1985 in the coastal city of Jeddah, Bayan's childhood was marked by a thirst for knowledge and a passion for justice. In a society where women were often relegated to the sidelines, she dared to dream of a different future, one where her voice and legal expertise could be used to empower others and fight for equality.

Overcoming societal norms and defying expectations, Bayan pursued her education with unwavering determination. She earned a degree in law from King Abdulaziz University and embarked on a training program that would equip her with the skills and experience necessary to navigate the complex world of legal practice.

In 2013, Bayan made history by becoming one of the first four women to be licensed as lawyers in Saudi Arabia. This momentous occasion marked a turning point in the kingdom's legal landscape, paving the way for other women to follow in her footsteps.

Undeterred by the challenges and uncertainties that lay ahead, Bayan set up her own law firm in 2014. This pioneering venture, the first all-female law firm in the country, was not just a business; it was a statement of defiance and a powerful symbol of female empowerment.

Through her legal practice, Bayan has dedicated herself to serving the community, advocating for the rights of individuals, and fighting for justice for all. She specializes in various legal areas, including family law, criminal law, and civil law, providing invaluable support and guidance to countless clients.

But Bayan's impact extends far beyond the courtroom. She is a vocal advocate for women's rights and actively participates in public dialogues and discussions aimed at promoting social reform and equality. Her voice resonates with women across the Arab world, inspiring them to challenge limitations and carve their own paths in a rapidly changing society.

Beyond her legal expertise and activism, Bayan is also a devoted mother and a role model for young women and girls.She embodies the perfect blend of ambition, compassion, and unwavering faith, demonstrating that success can be achieved without compromising on one's values or identity.

Bayan's story is not just a personal triumph; it is a collective victory for all those who strive for a more just and equitable world. Her journey serves as a beacon of hope, reminding us that even the most formidable barriers can be overcome with unwavering determination and a strong belief in oneself.

As Bayan continues to break down barriers and redefine what it means to be a Muslim woman in the 21st century, her legacy will continue to inspire future generations of women to dream big, challenge the status quo, and leave their own indelible mark on the world.

She is a trailblazer, a role model, and a symbol of hope. She is Bayan Mahmoud Al-Zahran, and her story is far from over.

Final Words

Dear Sisters, As you embark on the journey of entrepreneurship, remember that the path will be lined with both opportunities and challenges. Embrace each step with courage and faith, knowing that obstacles are not barriers but stepping stones to growth and learning.

One of the main challenges you may encounter is the uncertainty and risks inherent in starting and running a business. It is natural to feel apprehensive about the unknown. In these moments, turn to prayer and patience. Trust in your abilities and the wisdom you have gained from your experiences. Each decision, each risk taken, is a part of learning and evolving as an entrepreneur.

Financial constraints often present another significant hurdle. This reality tests not only your resourcefulness but also your resilience. It is important to plan meticulously, budget wisely, and remember that success does not always require substantial resources. Sometimes, the most impactful ideas stem from simplicity and creativity.

Balancing work and personal life is another aspect that requires your attention. There will be times when the demands of your business may overwhelm you. During these times, remember to take a step back and prioritize. Your health, both mental and physical, is crucial. Nurture it with the same dedication that you give to your business. Find solace in your family, your community, and your faith. They are your support system, your refuge in times of stress.

Facing societal expectations and stereotypes can be daunting. As a woman entrepreneur, you might encounter doubts and skepticism. Stand firm in your conviction and let your work speak for itself. Your success and determination will be a beacon for others to follow, challenging stereotypes and inspiring future generations.

In the face of these challenges, do not lose sight of your purpose and values. Let them be your guiding light. Seek counsel from those you trust, learn continuously, and stay open to feedback. Remember, every successful person has faced challenges, but what sets them apart is their perseverance and ability to learn from every situation.

Above all, hold onto your faith. It is your anchor in times of storm, your guide when the path seems unclear. With faith, patience, and determination, there is no obstacle too great to overcome.

Walk this path with grace and strength, knowing that you are capable, and your journey is a testament to your courage and faith.

May Allah guide your steps and bless your endeavors. Go forth and conquer, my sisters, the world awaits your brilliance.

Resources for Continuous Learning and Support

- Islamic Relief: Offers resources and training programs for Muslim entrepreneurs.

- The National Association of Muslim Professionals (NAMP): Provides networking opportunities and support for Muslim professionals and entrepreneurs.

- Muslimah Business Women Network: A global online community dedicated to empowering Muslim women entrepreneurs.

- Online courses and webinars: Numerous online resources offer valuable knowledge and skills development for entrepreneurs.

About The Author

Kirsten Evans, who embraced Islam in 2005 and adopted the name Ameena Evans, is a remarkable figure in the

South African business community. Her journey to Islam marked a significant turning point in her life, imbuing her endeavors with a profound sense of purpose and direction. Ameena has been a driving force behind several successful business ventures, showcasing her exceptional leadership and entrepreneurial skills.

Despite her achievements, she prefers to maintain a low profile, focusing on the substance of her work rather than personal publicity. This approach has earned her respect and admiration from her peers and employees alike.

Ameena's decision to write a book marks a new chapter in her already impressive career. Her book is not just a reflection of her business acumen; it's a heartfelt effort to reach out to fellow Muslim sisters, offering guidance and support. Through her writing, she shares the wisdom she has gained from her own experiences, both as a Muslim convert and a business leader. Her insights are especially valuable for those who navigate the complex intersection of faith, identity, and professional life.

In her book, Ameena addresses the unique challenges faced by Muslim women in the business world, offering practical advice on balancing religious obligations with career aspirations. She also delves into the nuances of conducting business ethically and successfully in a diverse and often challenging global landscape.

Overall, Ameena Evans' story is one of resilience, faith, and success. Her first book is a testament to her journey and a valuable resource for anyone looking to navigate the challenges of modern life while staying true to their beliefs and aspirations.

Contents